TROUBLEMAKER

TROUBLING WORDS FOR TROUBLED TIMES

Vicki Gray

*Jim —
superstar still.
Vicki*

A DEACON REFLECTS ON THE NEEDS, CONCERNS, AND HOPES OF THE WORLD

RED MOON PUBLICATIONS
Oklahoma City, OK 73120

Cover Art: Stained glass window in the Chapter House, St. George's Episcopal Cathedral, Jerusalem

Book Design: Lana B. Callahan, www.lbsdesignstudio.com

Library of Congress Control Number: 2013950078
ISBN 978-0-9851419-4-3

Printed in the United States of America

FOR MIMI

SOME VOICES OF INSPIRATION

"God requires us to act. We are called by our baptism to be moral leaders. We are required to go beyond moral authority and into the acts of moral leadership. To be a moral person, to be a moral Christian, a moral Episcopalian, to then to act on that moral authority and take moral leadership, requires sometimes, and more often than not, that we get into trouble, not stay out of trouble as the passive interpretation of morality would have us do (a moral person stays out of trouble). That is the way of the cross.

It is from Jesus, a servant leader, a troublemaker, that we take our moral leadership direction. And if we follow it, if we keep our baptismal promises, we are willingly vulnerable and we will get into trouble."

Bonnie Anderson, Past President, Episcopal House of Deputies, Sermon at Grace Cathedral, San Francisco, October 19, 2008

"There is a time when silence is betrayal."

Dr. Martin Luther King, Jr. (per Vincent Harding), "Beyond Vietnam" sermon, Riverside Church, April 4, 1967

"...if we have a voice we should use it...The Word we revere is not found in a book but in a voice. Our shared witness to what is true, what is good, what is right makes a difference. The prophetic is not the partisan. It is the universal cry of the common person speaking truth to power. It is the vision of community translated into the language of change. To be silent is to be silenced.

Bishop Steven Charleston, Hope As Old As Fire

"...If there is a danger in politicizing the faith...there is also a counter-danger, which is depoliticizing the faith. In times of oppression, if you don't translate choices of faith into political choices, you run the danger of washing your hands, like Pilate, and thereby, like Pilate, plaiting anew Christ's crown of thorns..."

William Sloane Coffin, Credo

"Institutions, no matter what they are, remain hollow if not accompanied by a charge to advocate for the people they are called to serve."

Grace Said, Palestine Israel Network, Episcopal Peace Fellowship

"That which the faithful find hardest to forgive is the unwillingness of their senior pastors to confront openly with them the problems they face in the world as it is today."

Morris West, A View from the Ridge

"If you are neutral in situations of injustice, you have chosen the side of the oppressor."

Archbishop Desmond Tutu

"A church that doesn't provoke any crises, a gospel that doesn't unsettle, a word of God that doesn't get under anyone's skin, a word of God that doesn't touch the real sin of the society in which it is being proclaimed — what gospel is that?"

Archbishop Oscar Romero

"In our era, the road to holiness necessarily passes through the world of action."

Dag Hammarskjold

"The worst attitude is indifference."
Stephane Hessel, *Time for Outrage*

"I often talk about faith as something that is personal, but never private. Each of us must take responsibility for the beliefs we hold and must personally wrestle with life's most fundamental questions. But once we have decided to follow Jesus, we cannot help but live out our personal beliefs in public ways."
Jim Wallis, *Sojourners*

ACKNOWLEDGMENTS

This project, like my lifetime of discernment, has required the help of many to whom I now offer my gratitude: Mr. Fitz, Father Novak, and those other Jesuits who planted the seed of a calling so long ago; Harold Clinehans and our sisters and brothers at St. Paul's who offered Mimi and me the refuge of their love; M.R. Ritley and Bill Countryman who gave me the courage to share my otherness; Fritz Jaentsch and others at Christ Church who lifted up both my otherness and my calling; Carol Saysette, Dorothy Jones, Anthony Turney, and Kate Salinaro who walked with me through dark valleys and sun-filled meadows; Rod Dugliss who introduced me anew to the prophets and opened to me their diaconal hermeneutic; Bill Swing who charged me always to preach what I believe and placed my cause in the comforting hands of the Holy Spirit; Marc Andrus who took a chance and made me a deacon in God's Church; the good people of St. James who first called me deacon; my brothers and sisters in Palestine who shared with me the pain of justice delayed; my homeless brothers and sisters at Open Cathedral who embedded in me a palpable understanding of the needs, concerns, and hopes of the world; Susan Champion who also understood and allowed me to speak my truth freely; my sisters and brothers at Christ the Lord who listened to my interpretations and urged me to seek a wider audience; Steven Charleston who offered me this vehicle to do so and urged me and everyone always to follow Jesus; all the prophets who still speak, especially Bonnie Anderson who taught me that to follow Jesus required one to be a troublemaker; and you who now hold these troubling words in your hands and, reading them, will hopefully also feel called to be troublemakers. Jesus needs you. So does the world.

PREFACE

These are troubled times.

In addressing them in the sermons on these pages, I recognize that my personal pain, frustration, and, yes, outrage have often bubbled up in ways that others might find troubling. I ask you, however, to look beyond my feelings and look instead through the lens of the diaconal hermeneutic at the needs, concerns, and hopes of a hurting world that need to be brought to the attention of the church and our several governments.

In my attempt to do that I have sought to avoid the senseless, futile lashing out at enemies real and imagined, recalling how, as in the case of Samson, that only brings the whole world crashing down on all of us...to no good end. I have sought instead to address the causes of our dis-ease and engage those responsible as well as those sitting silently on the sidelines in solutions that reflect both the thirst for justice and love of Jesus Christ without whom nothing can be accomplished.

In essence, then, these sermons are simply a call to live into our baptismal vows to proclaim by word and example the good news of God in Christ; to serve Christ in all persons, loving our neighbors as ourselves; and striving for justice and peace among all people, to respect the dignity of every human being. They recognize, indeed celebrate, that following Jesus in this fashion will, as Bonnie Anderson, our Past President of the Episcopal House of Deputies, has warned, get us into trouble. But that's the way it's 'spozed to be. We are called to be troublemakers. Jesus needs us. So does the world.

Where to begin? Might we do so by surveying the nature of our troubles? Might we begin with the seemingly endless wars we have been inured by...one war after another, each less worthy than the last...and one - Vietnam - that scarred my life and those of a whole generation of Vietnamese and Americans. And now, after a decade of killing, we're still trying to explain and extricate ourselves from our two longest wars, unnecessary "wars of choice" in Iraq and Afghanistan...wars that leave us facing perceived enemies on every continent and, around every corner, mired in fear, unable to face the obvious answer to our unasked question: "Why do they hate us?"

At home we suffer still the consequence of decades of the rampant greed and reckless risk-taking that produced a Great Recession in an America we hardly recognize any more...an America where we know the price of everything and the value of nothing.

And, in our pursuit of money, power, and total "security" against the vicissitudes of life in an imperfect world, we've been far too quick to jettison the remnants of our values - the values found in our Baptismal Covenant and Constitution - and, for that, have paid an awful price. In this regard, another question - John le Carre's - also begs an answer: "How far can we go in the rightful defense of our Western values without abandoning them along the way?"[1] As the dismal moral record of the last decade - torture, rendition, "black sites," drones, "targeted assassinations," Guantanamo - suggests, apparently very far indeed. And, from the Christians in the room, one might make out the sad, faint whisper "Too far."

In our hundreds of thousands we marched against the wars. In the camps of Occupy we expressed our outrage at the greed and increasing inequality. With growing futility we voted, only to find our voices muffled by money. At countless demonstrations we raised the cry "No justice! No peace!" "No justice! No peace!" And, in that cry, we heard the ancient prophets' plea not for the mere absence of violence, the silent peace of the graveyard, but, rather, for the peace of Shalom that rests on justice and that encompasses a shared sense of well-being in the community.

But, for too long now that sense of justice and shared well-being has eluded us. The powers-that-be of this world still stand athwart the need for change - banks that gambled with our savings and took our homes, corporations that export our jobs, politicians who spout focus-group-tested one-liners and fiddle while a nation burns, a corporate media that would distract us from the fire with daily offerings of circus-like "infotainment." The results are an income inequality not seen since 1928, in which 40 percent of the nation's wealth is held by one percent of our people; real unemployment near 16 percent; an increasingly less progressive tax system unworthy of a civilized society; rampant cuts in programs for the suffering among us; in sum, a people on their knees.

The prospects are daunting but, with faith and hope and love, nowhere near insurmountable.

We are at a crossroads and the stakes are high. We need just get off our knees and find our voices.

As people of faith and as Americans, we are a people of hope. We must give voice to our longings and aspirations. As Martin Luther King, Jr. said about a war, "A time comes when silence is betrayal."[2] That time has come again in America. We are at another moment when silence is betrayal. Our old ways of doing things no longer work. We must find new ways…new ways that reflect our faith in God and our concern for one another.

As people of faith we must now speak truth to power - on Wall Street and in Washington - and stand in solidarity with those who seek peace and a more equitable society. Mindful that we are called, in the words of Micah, "to do justice, and to love kindness, and to walk humbly with your God,"[3] let us do so strengthened by the promise of Jesus that "Blessed are those who hunger and thirst for righteousness, for they will be filled."[4]

Mindful also, as Walter Rauschenbusch said, that such righteousness is "not a matter of getting of getting individuals to heaven, but of transforming life on earth into the harmony of heaven," we must insist that "the highest type of goodness is that which puts freely at the service of the community all that man is and can be" and that conversely, "the highest type of badness is that which uses up the wealth and happiness and virtue of the community to please self."[5]

As people of faith, we must seek a seat at the table and help shape solutions consistent with our values of justice, equality, charity, and solidarity with our fellow human beings. We must not shy from the political fray, for both politics and religion concern themselves with social relationships, how we relate to one another, how we will shape our societies. Good politics, like good religion, seeks to shape a just society.

Finally, we must be diligent in our efforts and impatient with those who would temporize. In the words of Martin Luther King, "Human progress never rolls in on wheels of inevitability; it comes through the tireless efforts of men willing to be co-workers with God, and without this hard work, time itself becomes an ally of the forces of social stagnation. We must use time creatively, in the knowledge that the time is always ripe to do right. Now is the time to make real the promise of democracy."[6]

Only when we redeem that promise - and that of the Gospel - will we enjoy the true peace of Shalom.

So how do we do that?

We must begin by being witnesses. We must be honest, authentic witnesses to God's suffering people in a suffering world. That is not something that can be done by reading a book or from a distance. It requires us to go out to where the people are and listen to their pain. It requires us to leave our buildings - our homes and churches - to stand in solidarity with those we would help and to speak loudly to those we would petition on their behalf. A witness must be seen and heard

As Pope Francis said, "We need to 'go out'…to the 'outskirts' where there is suffering, bloodshed, blindness that longs for sight, and prisoners in thrall to many evil masters." We need to "go out and give ourselves and the Gospel to others, giving what little ointment we have to those who have nothing, nothing at all."[7]

For my part, I have sought to share what little ointment I have ministering to the homeless on the streets of San Francisco, those in the San Francisco Jail, immigrants facing deportation and family separation, underpaid and abused hotel and domestic workers, cancer patients at UCSF Mt. Zion, my transgendered brothers and sisters, and my brothers and sisters further afield - Palestinians, Cubans, Central Americans - who are suffering oppression and economic deprivation and exploitation. Though I have done both, I am acutely aware that ministry is more than writing a check or saying a prayer. It requires going to the "outskirts' of society to its dark and dingy corners where the suffering, bloodshed, and spiritual numbness are tangible, palpable…and shared.

But we need also to recognize that charity, while always necessary, is never sufficient. If we are really serious about "transforming life on earth into the harmony of heaven," we must advocate for the justice that requires systemic change. I am reminded in this regard of a sermon about the Good Samaritan by the Rev. Katherine Ward, rector emerita of St. Augustine's, Oakland. It was good and necessary, she said, to help the man in the ditch who had been set upon by bandits on that notoriously dangerous Jericho Road. But, having done that, she added, the Samaritan should have turned to petitioning the authorities in Jerusalem to make the road safe for future travelers.

We must move beyond just treating the consequences of a sick society and attack the causes of the illness. We must also move beyond - build upon - personal morality to seek communal well-being. We must give the poor not just a handout, but a voice, recalling that the meaning of *advocare* is to "give voice to."

And, having done so, we must report the unvarnished, uncomfortable truth of our experience of the world to all who would listen, especially those still huddled behind church walls. As Albert Einstein once said, "The right to search for the truth implies also a duty; one must not conceal any part of what one has recognized to be the truth."[8]

That can often prove uncomfortable and sometimes lead to being called names or ostracized. I recall standing on the Mount of Beatitudes, my back to the Sea of Galilee, and being asked to comment on the Beatitudes for the group of pilgrims with whom I had just visited the wall and ring of settlements surrounding Bethlehem, the segregated streets of Hebron, the refugee camps, and locked-down towns and villages of the West Bank. When we got to Matthew 5:11 ("Blessed are you when people revile you and…"), I warned my fellow travelers that, when we got home and spoke the truth about what we had experienced in Israel/Palestine, we would be called names (as, indeed, we were) and urged them to cling to the promise in the "blessed" that introduced the verse.

That said, those who have a pulpit must use it…to preach the truth as they have experienced it, however uncomfortable or troubling it might be… and recognizing that the words spoken may be even more uncomfortable and troubling for the speaker than to those upon whose ears they fall. You want trouble? How about that sermon by Jesus in that synagogue in Nazareth, after which the congregants chased him to a cliff and wanted to throw him off?

But we are called to follow Jesus to that cliff's edge. Again, as Bonnie Anderson, has said, "It is from Jesus, a servant leader, a troublemaker, that we take our moral leadership direction. And if we follow it, if we keep our baptismal promises, we are willingly vulnerable and we will get into trouble."[9]

The imperfect sermons on these pages are but the effort of one deacon to live into her ordination vow "to interpret to the church the needs, concerns, and hopes of the world"…to bring to the church her experience of the world. Mindful of the duty invoked by Einstein and the admonition of one bishop to "always preach what you believe" I have welcomed the vulnerability and trouble that sometimes entails. Confident, however, that, in following Jesus the Troublemaker, I am on safe ground, I often feel like I am driving around in a pick-up truck with a "No Fear" decal on the window of the cab. And, at my age, what is there to fear?

Age brings also a sense of that "fierce urgency of now." My time to effect change is increasingly limited and I feel a pressing need to recruit new troublemakers. At the same time, I find that my capacity for outrage at the obvious nature of the injustices and indignities being visited upon so many knows no limits. I have neither the time nor the temperament for temporizing or obfuscation…or simply paraphrasing the clear words of the Evangelists the faithful have just heard. Nor would I insult the intelligence of those to whom I would speak. I prefer instead to use the words of the Gospel as a take-off point "to confront openly with them the problems they face in the world as it is today."[10]

Too often and too easily, however, I have found, the urgency of my outrage bubbles over in sometimes troubling ways to anger. That is something I struggle with on the pages of my journal and in my prayer life. Indeed, I have to struggle to carve out time for prayer and reflection…to savor the little joys of life that are so necessary to maintaining balance and hope. And every truly Christian homily must end with hope, for it is Good News that is being conveyed…the promise that all will be well.

But, still, along the way, I've found myself turning again and again to Jesus the Troublemaker, the outraged, angry Jesus who kicked over the tables of the moneychangers in the vestibule of the Temple and called out its priests as hypocrites presiding over a profaned institution. And I've found this Jesus in less obvious places…in, for example, Mark 1:40-45, where Jesus, "moved with pity," cured a leper. In my sermon on that reading for Epiphany Six 2009, however, I chose the alternative translation that has Jesus "moved with anger"…anger at the indignity of the leper's situation and turned again against the priestly establishment.

My reasons for that choice as for others in these homilies had less to do with my rusty knowledge of Greek (gained long ago in a Jesuit high school) than with my lived experience. As I said one Epiphany Sunday, when "confronted by similar situations on the streets of San Francisco, I've always found 'pity' much too weak a word, an all too condescending attitude, an unworthy emotion, an inadequate response to what I see as a systemic failure - the failure of our society and government to care for the weakest among us. No, I usually respond - to myself and to God - with anger at how we as a community have failed to "respect the dignity of every human being."

I used to feel guilty about that, but no longer. Sometimes, I've found, it's okay to be angry. As Obery Hendricks, Jr. writes in *The Politics of Jesus*:

> Jesus' response shows us that there are things we should be angry about, there are things we must say and do as a testimony against every action, system, policy, and institution that excludes any of God's children from the fullest fruits of life for any reason. That is to say, we must endeavor to love everyone, but we must also take sides. We cannot be against injustice if we do not take the side of justice. We must be angered by the mistreatment of any of God's children. When we see people hurt and excluded in the name of God, we should be angry.[11]

That is the sort of anger that can be found in so many of the sermons on these pages and for which I beg, if not your forgiveness, your understanding. In turn, I offer mine…my understanding that anger is not enough. It can motivate and move. But it cannot achieve. It cannot achieve that Kingdom we seek "on earth as it is in heaven." For that, we need hope and, above all, love, without which we would be but that "noisy gong" or "clanging cymbal."

Not wishing to be either, let me offer you my love on our shared journey…and the hope that grows from faith in Christ.

BY WAY OF INTRODUCTION

A SPEECH

FROM DESTROYER DECK TO PULPIT

Once upon a time - actually, twice upon a time - I ran for city council in Vallejo. I had been energized by the efforts to save Mare Island. I lost, but Mare Island won…and so did we.

During my campaigns, one of my flyers asked "Who is Vicki Gray?" Having read it, one lady exclaimed "Your life reads like Forrest Gump's - always in the company of great people, on the edge of great events!" Yes, I did march with Martin. I did earn a Bronze Star in the Mekong Delta. In the Department of State, I did brief Secretaries of State and Presidents. I did earn a Ph.D and teach at the National Defense University. And once I was a man.

But you know all that. Is that, however, all there is to Vicki Gray? To any person? A resume…of things we did? Are we what we do? Or who we are?

Those are all questions that were swirling in my head when Myrna asked me to speak today and say something about myself and a life so shaped by the Navy and the Church. And, so, the title: "From Destroyer Deck to Pulpit." It's a title I cribbed - shamelessly - from Martin Niemoeller, a World War I submarine commander who became a leader of the Confessing Church in Hitler's Germany. On the eve of being sent off to Dachau, he wrote a book called *From Submarine to Pulpit.*[12] He has always been a hero of mine.

Another hero of mine and one of my favorite theologians is the Greek

A speech delivered on May 14, 2007 at St. Peter's Chapel, Mare Island, Vallejo, California on the occasion of the annual Daffodil Tea to raise funds to preserve St. Peter's Chapel.

poet Nikos Kazantzakis. Toward the close of his autobiography, *Report to Greco*, he describes "three kinds of souls, three kinds of prayers. One: I am a bow in your hands, lord. Draw me lest I rot. Two: Do not overdraw, Lord. I shall break. Three: Overdraw me, and who cares if I break! Choose!"[13] I guess I fall into the third category, though the choices were not mine, but God's.

Today, I'd like to talk about those choices - God's choices - the events, the strains, the losses - that have made me - for better or for worse - who I am.

Again, I've done a lot of exciting things, participated in small ways in big events, and had my share of worldly accomplishments. But far more important than what I've won is what I've lost. As I'm sure many of you have also experienced, we become - we are - what is taken away from us. As we go through life - if we are honest - we find ourselves being peeled… like an onion or an artichoke. And - if we are lucky - we are like one of those brightly colored Panamanian molas in the hands of God, allowing God to cut through life's accretions, always leaving what's important of each layer, but cutting through relentlessly, skillfully, to the core, the heart, the essence of what we are intended to be - something bright and beautiful.

In my case, God has cut deep and with sometimes wild abandon. I've lost a lot. In Vietnam, I lost my innocence. Then I found and lost the love of my life. And, toward the end of her life, I lost myself, or, at least, a great part of myself. But, in the process, I developed a sense of what was important, what had to be held onto. I leave it to you - and to God - to judge whether what I held onto is worthwhile, bright, or beautiful.

At the start, I didn't think about such things. Isn't that always the way of youth, so full of innocence and optimism? Growing up in the Bronx wasn't always easy. We weren't rich and I wasn't very healthy. But I did go to a good school - Fordham Prep -and, after the Naval Academy, escaped to a life at sea on the deck of a destroyer.

But, even then, the clouds were gathering - our national struggle with civil rights and my personal struggle with my gender identity. They both demanded attention. Then came Vietnam, a cloud, it seemed with silver linings. I would make the world safe for democracy and prove to the world and to myself, that I was a man…and a damn tough one at that.

Oh, I was tough. The Bronze Star citation says so. But Vietnam, like any war, was never like a John Wayne movie. My narrow world of jungle canals was more like "Apocalypse Now," a dark nightmare that still sends shivers up my spine. Death - up close - has a way of doing that.

Two weeks after I got there - to Long Phu or, as I call it, "the place I learned to cry" - my counterpart was killed, shot between the eyes at pointblank range. Worse yet, I had already killed my first human being and, soon, the killing became a blur.

There was, however, one death I will never forget. We had received a lot of fire from a notorious island - Cu Lao Dung. I called in an airstrike and soon the shriek of the jet was followed by a series of thuds, bright orange balls of flame, and black clouds that reeked of gasoline. Then, in what has become a recurring personal nightmare, a young woman emerged from the stinking black cloud of burning napalm we had just unleashed, paddling toward us in a sampan,. We stopped her. Caked with mud and soot and tears, she looked much older than her years. Reaching into the bottom of the boat, she held up a tiny chunk of something - black, still smoking - the remnants of her baby. She broke down shrieking - growling - to God and to us! The sound still rattles in my head.

But Vietnam also brought me a far happier dream - a dream of love. It began one September Saturday in 1965, when Vic, a young naval officer on his way to Vietnam, encountered Mimi, a school teacher, four years younger. We fell madly in love.

"Thank God for Vietnam," I've often thought, for it left me with a stack of letters - hers and mine - that attest to the authenticity and urgency of young love. Just weeks after my return to "the world" we were married in Carmel on January 7, 1967. Over the years, neither of us forgot the clarity of each other's smiles that day or the honesty of our shared vow - "Till death do we part."

It was a vow that was tested by the same familiar trials that millions of married couples endure. They were trials, however, that were trumped by a full measure of happiness, adventure, and worldly "accomplishment." We travelled the world and dined and danced with presidents and movie stars, and lived, in every way, abundant lives.

It would have been wonderful to grow old together, to live "happily ever after." But such endings happen more often in fairy tales and B movies than in real life, and, what passes for happiness is, as often as not, ephemeral tinsel. Our epiphany of that truth came much too early or, as we later thought, just in time. For, in the *real* tests that followed, we found salvation and produced something beautiful.

Those real tests were life-threatening, life-changing, and, ultimately, life-affirming. They were breast cancer and something called gender identity dysphoria. The latter - my confusion - was something we struggled with together for much of our married life. Mimi's cancer overtook us much more suddenly - on an April morning in 1988. They were tests that intertwined and defined our last dozen years together. We found ourselves engaged in prolonged grieving, having to say "Goodbye" to each other in multiple ways.

Making our way "home" to California in the midst of it all, we found ourselves at St. Paul's in Benicia. Mimi was recovering from chemo-induced heart failure, and I, still "in the closet," was embarked on the final stages of the transsexual journey. We knew there would be more, traumatic changes, but, for the moment, felt secure in a church that brought us the solace of a loving family, and a pastor, Harold Clinehens, who stretched our spiritual envelope. Our "outing" could wait…or so we thought.

But we were being pressed - by the growing intensity of my obsession; the growing, self-destructive depths of the depression that accompanied it; the growing need to be honest with family and friends; and the growing sense that our time to do so was limited. We prayed and cried together and determined we would share our truth. We could do no less with those we loved, and, given a new found understanding of Grace, knew we had nothing to fear.

And, so the unfolding began. Each step of the way, it became easier to begin with the simple, declarative "I am a transsexual." So, we began, our disclosure to Mimi's mom, Adrienne, who replied, relieved it seemed, "Oh, that's not so bad; I was afraid you were getting divorced." And, then, there was my Ash Wednesday confession to Father Harold, who replied "I don't see any sin in this," adding honestly, "I don't understand it, but we'll work our way through it together." And we did…together.

I remember vividly my first day at church as Vicki. You want guts?! Mimi had them, as she walked before me to communion. It was a breeze for me, thereafter. Mimi was always there before me; I sensed Christ there behind me; and we all smiled on the way back. Mimi was there, too, that morning, when in our prayer group, someone insisted on speaking his mind about my "sin." She held my hand, as I held his, as he read from his Bible about how I was an "abomination." I will never forget the trembling and perspiration of his hand and the coolness and firmness of Mimi's.

The loss of Vic was not easy for Mimi, or for me. We both grieved his quickening disappearance. For Mimi, Vicki was never an adequate substitute for Vic, but she was always there, each step of the way, supporting me as a wife, teaching me as an "older," wiser sister, loving me as a friend and soulmate. And, in the vulnerability of her own illness, she unknowingly kept me from feeling sorry for myself, from imploding into the self-centeredness that afflicts too many transgendered people. She was always there to allow me to care for her…as she cared for me. And, together, we incarnated an "issue." "Here is transsexuality," we said. "Touch us. Feel us. Interact with us. Above all, love us, as we love you."

And Mimi and I loved each other, too…till the very end. As she lay dying, I said a lot of inane things. And, selfish to the end, I asked, "Do you still love me?" All she could manage through her morphine haze was "Uh huh." But that was enough! I pressed her hand. She smiled. We had kept our vow.

Toward the end of our life together - Mimi's and mine - I got to know the British writer Jan Morris, also transgendered, and her beloved Elizabeth. In Conundrum, she said of their marriage: "It was a marriage that had no right to work, yet it worked like a dream, living testimony, one might say, to the power of mind over matter - or of love in its purest sense over everything else."[14] Nor did ours have a right to work. But it continues to work - like a dream - in those shared dreams that we - Mimi and I - retreat to each night. (Am I in hers or is she in mine?) And, in those love-filled dreams, I sense eternity.

Mimi died on an April afternoon - much like today. It was 2000. God had cut this mola to the core. There was nothing left to reveal. I had reached an end of sorts - a bottom - a widow now, Mimi's ring upon a necklace, no one to care for, not knowing what to do, waiting. For what?

The next summer, I set out on a two-month search for answers - a Celtic pilgrimage to rocky cliffs and islands on Ireland's westernmost edges and to the very top of Scotland. I visited lots of beautiful - and empty - churches, but found God strong and well in the most god-awful places. And, in myself, I found new strength and purpose.

There had to be more to life and church than what I found when I returned. It was September 2001. The shared grief we all endured that second week and the death of a dear young friend a month later shook me hard. I found myself shaking my fist at heaven and shouting "What in the hell are you doing up there!" No I didn't *hear* the response, But I felt it. It seemed to say: "Quit the whining! Life is tough. Get on with it."

And get on with it I did. I soon found myself at the Episcopal School for Deacons at Berkeley and, after a long and arduous process of discernment and affirmation, I was ordained last December at Grace Cathedral. As a result of that and my various ministries in San Francisco, I've faded somewhat from Vallejo's struggles. Now you can find me at St. James in the Richmond neighborhood of San Francisco - doing this - preaching. You can also find me with the ladies of Pod D in the San Francisco Jail, among the chemo patients at UCSF Mt. Zion, and, if you were there last Sunday, leading morning prayer on Justin Hermann Plaza.

Life is rich and life is good. And, toward the end, I can report, like that Greek poet, "I am full of wounds and still standing on my feet. Full of wounds, all in the breast, I did what I could...."[15]

And, at the end, I will report - what more can any of us say - "I tried."

THE SERMONS

A SERMON UPON THE INSTALLATION
OF THE NIGHT MINISTER

In the name of Jesus Christ, you are to serve all people, particularly the poor, the weak, the sick, and the lonely...You are to make Christ and his redemptive love known by your word and example, to those among whom you live, and work, and worship. You are [also] to interpret to the Church the needs, the concerns, and hopes of the world.[16]

These words are from the rubric for the ordination of a deacon in the Book of Common Prayer. They speak to all Christians - be they English Catholics, German Catholics, or garden variety Roman Catholics - to how we are called to live from the moment of our Baptismal Covenant. In the Book of Common Prayer that Covenant ends with two questions:

Will you seek and serve Christ in all persons, loving your neighbor as yourself?

Will you strive for justice and peace among all people, and respect the dignity of every human being?

Having answered - hopefully loud and strong - "I will, with God's help," we all became ministers - ministers engaged in the two-fold task of bringing love and justice to all God's people - to the poor, the weak, the sick, the marginalized like me, and, I would add, the wealthy, the strong, and the healthy, who can be just as lonely and in need of hope as anyone else - especially in the dark that is the middle of the night. Love and

Installation of The Rev. Lyle Beckman as San Francisco Night Minister, St. Mark's Lutheran Church, San Francisco, May 20, 2007

justice…and hope.

But, how to proceed? In Matthew, Jesus reminds us: "Just as you did it to one of the least of these who are members of my family, you did it to me."[17] And, in his letter to the Colossians, Paul advises us to clothe ourselves with the love that binds us all together in harmony and to internalize the peace of Christ in our hearts which beat as one in one body.

In unpacking all this, we confront several words and concepts - love, justice, unity, harmony, peace - words and concepts that come together in the biblical term **Shalom**. Too often we translate *shalom* simply as "peace." But peace in the sense of shalom encompasses justice, a sense of well-being, of rightness, of the state of being intended by God…as in "the way it's spozed to be." Shalom is God's peace which is based on justice. "No justice, no peace!" How many times have you heard that mantra shouted in anger at one rally or another? But how much easier it would be to achieve both - justice and peace - if we sought them not in anger but in love.

For his part, Isaiah sees his task - our task - as seeking justice. He seeks "to loose the bonds of injustice, to undo the thongs of the yoke, to let the oppressed go free, and to break every yoke."[18] But, he tells us, we must seek do so with love, sharing our bread, opening our doors to the homeless, clothing the naked. Why? Not because it's a nice thing to do. Not because it makes us feel good…or better than those with whom we share. Not because we are privileged to give from some surplus out of some sense of *noblesse oblige* –to give something we'd hardly miss. No, we must share in the sense of digging deep, of fasting till it hurts, of giving the very coat off our backs, of sharing the hunger and chill endured by our brothers and sisters, *because we are kin*. We are all, as Jesus tells us, "members of my family." We are all one body. We are all in this together.

I have always found "charity" or *caritas* to be a deficient, stingy translation of the word "love," when what Jesus meant was the familial love, the solidarity of *agape*. We must not, as Isaiah says, hide ourselves from our kin.

Indeed, we must give ourselves - our time, our energy, our willingness to relate not as some dispenser of charity, but as equals, as brothers and sisters to all our kin. Far more important than any *thing* we can give - food, clothing, housing - is the simple recognition of the dignity we all share as members of God's family. It is the ministry of presence and witness - to witness the presence of Christ among us and in us.

And it is just *that* that the ministers of the Night Ministry - Lyle, Don, Chuck, the assistant night ministers, the crisis line counselors, and all of you who support the ministry - do so uniquely well with the people we encounter every night in a doorway on the street, at a coffee counter, on a bar stool, or on the other, darkened end of a phone line. What a gift to look someone in the eye, to listen attentively - actively - to the other's story, to touch one another, and to mean it when we say "We are family."

For my part, I've always found it a reciprocal gift. Meditating on Matthew's Gospel, we're wont to seek the face of Christ in the "least" of those in our family. But, how often I've wondered do others see the face of Christ in me or number me among the "least."

And, always - on the street or on the phone - I've learned, above all, that "presence" means listening - hard, intently, compassionately. That ability to listen actively is probably the biggest lesson I have learned from my brief time with the Night Ministry. No wonder Don Stuart's book on his time as Night Minister is entitled *I'm Listening as Fast as I Can*. In it, Don writes:

> It was not my objective to "preach" to street people in the usual sense. This was a ministry of presence, and presence at a time inconvenient for the traditional church to respond. It was stemming the flow of blood from slashed wrists or from a beating. It was sharing the "Good News" through being there when no one else was, and at any time of the night…I didn't mark the success of my nights by counting up how many souls I had "saved" or how many new members I had added to the church rolls. I simply planted seeds. If the people couldn't see that the

love of God was being shared with them through a tired and soaking-wet clergyman coming at two or three o'clock on a rainy morning, they would hardly hear my words.[19]

How like my own response to a secular friend in Vallejo, who asked with a tinge of sarcasm about my time on the streets "How many souls have you saved?" My response was "I don't think of it in terms of saving souls, but rather of giving people hope, perhaps barely enough hope to make it through the night to the first rays of dawn."

There's a pregnant, hopeful quality about the middle of the night, be it in a Middle Eastern hovel or in this 9-to-5 capital of finance and commerce. Listen to Dom Helder Camara, that Brazilian saint of the impoverished, as he writes about how Jesus came to us in the midnight of the year and how often he bursts into our lives again and again - suddenly, unexpectedly - in the midnights of our lives. Listen these to words from Helder Camara's "It's Midnight, Lord:"

> In the middle of the night.
> When stark night was darkest,
> then you chose to come.
>
> God's resplendent first-born
> sent to make us one.
>
> If you had been afraid of shadows
> You would have been born at noon.
> But you preferred the night.
>
> Lord, you were born in the middle of the night
> because midnight is pregnant with dawn.
> The darker the night
> the more joyful the dawn;
> the deadly past is dead

when the sun is reborn –
precious present, gift of now.

It's true, Lord,
it is the deepest midnight.

But how can we forget
that the darker is the night,
the lovelier dawn.

All this relates to the first part of that charge to deacons I began with - "to serve all people…[and] to make Christ and his redemptive love known."

But, being a deacon, I cannot forget the second charge: "to interpret to the Church the needs, the concerns, and hopes of the world."

By my lights, the Night Minister, the Night Ministry - and all of us - must do both. We must treat the consequences of societal evil and we must draw attention its causes.

Yes, we must "stem the flow of blood from slashed wrists or from a beating." But we must also seek to restrain the hand of those who would beat down our brothers and sisters. And we should not allow ourselves to be deterred by those who would call us names for doing so. Dom Helder Camara also wrote: "When I give food to the poor, they call me a saint. When I ask why the poor have no food, they call me a communist." To which Jesus would surely reply "Not to worry, for 'blessed are you when people revile you and persecute you and utter all kinds of evil against you falsely on my account.'"

Someone else who was called names in his time was William Sloane Coffin. Before he died last year Coffin was Senior Minister at Riverside Church and is immortalized as Reverend Sloan in "Doonsbury." Concerning the duality of our task - the need for both charity **and** justice - he said:

Perhaps the crucial question is this: Is charity ever a

substitute for justice? I've listened to many a Marxist accuse the churches of having a vested interest in unjust structures that produce victims to whom good Christians can then pour out their hearts in charity. I've listened and shuddered, because so often in history its been so true... If there is a danger in politicizing the faith...there is also a counter danger, which is depoliticizing the faith. In times of oppression, if you don't translate choices of faith into political choices, you run the danger of washing your hands, like Pilate,and thereby, like Pilate, plaiting anew Christ's crown of thorns for "in as much as ye did it unto the least of these my brethren, ye did it unto me." In scripture, there is no purely spiritual answer to slavery; no purely spiritual answer to the pain of the poor, nor the arrogance of tyrants.[21]

I hope, therefore, that Lyle and all of us associated with the Night Ministry will not only continue to "serve all people, particularly the poor, the weak, the sick, and the lonely," but also to interpret to the Church and the world the needs, the concerns, and hopes of those very people who too often in this city are voiceless and hidden from view.

Let us not just stand with them and listen to them on Eddy, Polk, or Haight, but also ensure they are seen and heard in City Hall, in the media, and in our churches.

It is time, as Caryll Houselander has said,

for Christians [to] put aside their self-protective type of religion with its interminable formalities and careful exclusions and respectable cliques and recognize Christ and themselves in the disreputable members of the church, the socially ostracized; the repulsive, the criminals, the insane, the drifting population of the man or woman waiting in the condemned cell to die - and the tiresome, thankless members of a man or woman's own household.

It is time that Christians answered Cain's question, 'Am I my brother's (or sister's) keeper' with more than a [simple] affirmative, [but rather]: 'I am more than that - I *am* my brother and my sister.'[22]

If we can so answer, we have been promised that our "light shall break forth like the dawn," our "healing shall spring up quickly," and, when we call for help, the Lord will answer "Here I am."

AMDG[23]

A TIME TO LEAVE
A FAREWELL SERMON ON LUKE 9:57-62 2008

"As they went on their way, a man said to Jesus, 'I will follow you wherever you go." Jesus said to him, 'Foxes have holes, and birds have their nests, but the Son of Man has nowhere to lie down and rest.'"[24]

He might have added "Still want to follow?"

"He said to another man, 'Follow me.' But the man said, 'Sir, first let me go back and bury my father.' Jesus answered, 'Let the dead bury their own dead. You go and proclaim the Kingdom of God."

Still want to follow?

"Someone else said, 'I will follow you, sir, but first let me go and say goodbye to my family.' Jesus said to him, 'Anyone who starts to plow then keeps looking back is of no use to the Kingdom of God."

Still want to follow? It's a question I've often pondered, as I've read this passage. And, as I've done so, I've had to ask, "Does Jesus, our fully human brother, understand how difficult his words are? The magnitude of what he's asking?" Drop everything! Forget about your father, your mother, family, friends. Don't ask to lie down and rest. Don't ask where we're going. Just follow!

How hard. How very hard. And how I've resisted. I too want to rest in family and friends. Like others - perhaps you - I've begged off time and again. "Why me?" I've objected time and again. And, again and again, I've

Upon leaving St. James, San Francisco, in August 2008, after three years as intern and deacon.

39

heard a familiar voice - that *Hound of Heaven* [25]– "There's work to be done. No time to rest. Don't get comfortable."

But - no matter how hard I've resisted - I've always found irresistible the tug to move on whenever I start feeling comfortable. For me, comfort signals danger - the danger of growing accustomed to some happiness, in which case diminished intensity always threatens the dullness of salt that's lost its taste. But Nikos Kazantzakis, the Greek Nobel Laureate poet, points to an even greater danger - the danger of *not* growing accustomed to one's happiness. Of that danger, he writes, "I would always consider it as great as before, in which case I would be lost completely. I saw a bee drowned in its honey once, and learned my lesson."[26]

And so, in the happiness and comfort of this community of family and friends that is St. James, I feel the need to move on, to continue the journey that for all of us is life's pilgrimage, to do the work I feel called to do in an ever-widening circle. Nothing earthly can long remain static, unchanged. Indeed, "For everything there is a season, and a time for every matter under heaven." There is "a time to embrace, and a time to refrain from embracing"…a time to join a community and a time to leave.

For me that time to leave has come…after three years of happiness and comfort in your embrace. I find it necessary for my spiritual health and hope that you will forgive my selfishness in this regard. But, necessary though I might find it, it is for me a source of great grief. I've had many departures and far too many farewells in my life. But they never get easier. Saying "Goodbye" to your family is never easy. I'm only glad that, unlike the young man in our Gospel story, Mary Moore and you have given me this opportunity to do that…to say "Goodbye."

But despite the grief of leaving friends and leaving home there's always the excitement of new adventure, the lure of the unknown, the urgency of the call. Listen again to Kazantzakis:

Once more the wind of embarkment blew across my mind. How long would it continue to do so? God grant until mydeath! What joy to cast off from dry land and depart!

To snip the string that ties us to certitude and depart! To
look behind us and see the men and mountains we love
receding into the distance.[27]

Once upon a time, I watched those mountains on Kazantzakis' Crete
recede into the distance behind the wake of a sleek gray ship. And last
month, making the rough voyage over a gray sea from Iona to Staffa, I felt
again the spirit of Columba, Brendan, and all those other Celtic monks who
set out across that Western Sea to follow Christ, to seek God.

Once more the wind of embarkment blew across my mind. And so it
does today. I guess I'm just a restless soul, doomed perhaps - or maybe
blessed - to keep moving across this metaphorical sea called life, infected,
entranced, by what John Masefield called "Sea Fever:"

I must go down to the seas again, for the call
of the running tide
Is a wild call and a clear call that may not bedenied;
And all I ask is a windy day with the white
clouds flying,
And the flung spray and the blown spume, and
the sea-gulls crying.[28]

Even now, I can taste the saltiness of that spray, feel its cold sting,
inhale the aroma of iodine. It promises the adventure of new challenges.
But life, like any sea, also threatens danger.

I'm convinced, however, that, as long as you keep your eye on that
Western horizon - the kingdom of God that beckons - and a steady hand
on the tiller, there is really nothing to fear. Our Psalm today - my favorite
- tells us so:

If I take the wings of the morning
and settle at the farthest limits of
the sea,
even there your hand shall lead me,
and your right hand shall hold me
fast.[29]

When I was a far younger person, I carried with me a pocket version of Thomas a Kempis' *Imitation of Christ*. I carried it with me across strange seas…to even stranger lands. And this week I had occasion to open its mildewed pages once again, as I pondered Christ's words in today's Gospel: "Foxes have holes, and birds have their nests, but the Son of Man has nowhere to lie down and rest."

What sort of life is this we're called to imitate? Think about the life of Jesus…the nature of his ministry. From the moment of his Baptism in the Jordan to his last breath on the cross, Jesus was constantly on the go, always moving, never resting…except to pray in solitude for renewed strength for the journey. He didn't build any churches. He preached to people wherever he found them - in existing churches or, rather, synagogues; in their homes; and in the streets. And he sent his disciples - into the unknown - to do the same, without food or supplies, without any guarantee of success, dependant totally on the hospitality of the people they met. "You go," he said, "and proclaim the Kingdom of God."

That, of course, is what we're all called to do in our Baptismal vows. Remember that third Baptismal question? "Will you proclaim by word and example the Good News of God in Christ?" And, surely, you recall our answer: "I will with God's help."

I have tried to do that here and I will try, with God's help - and your blessing - to do so elsewhere. And, as I have tried to do here, I will always remember that that Good News is incredibly, blessedly simple: "God is love, and those who abide in love abide in God, and God abides in them."

And so I'll leave you with that - that simple message - God is love. I leave you my love and, I pray, take with me yours.

AMDG

NAKBA
A SERMON FOR ADVENT TWO 2008

"Comfort, comfort my people says your God. Speak tenderly to Jerusalem and say to her that her warfare is ended, that her iniquity is pardoned, that she has received from the Lord's hand double for all her sins.

A voice cries: 'In the wilderness prepare the way of the Lord, make straight in the desert a highway for our God.'" [30]

So begins our reading from Isaiah, this Jerusalem Sunday, our second Sunday of Advent.

On the eve of Advent, as some of you know, I visited Jerusalem and rode up that highway through the desert wilderness of Palestine. And, like Isaiah, everywhere I went throughout the occupied West Bank - Biblical Judea and Samaria - I found a moral wilderness; some people - Israeli settlers - its proud new lords; others –the oppressed Palestinians - confused, confounded, and nearly devoid of hope. It was a shock I hadn't prepared for or anticipated.

True enough, I knew that our team of 22 Christian witnesses, most from around the Bay Area, were going to Palestine to mark the 60th anniversary of what the Palestinians call the *Nakba* or Catastrophe - the destruction of

First sermon at Christ the Lord Episcopal Church, Pinole, CA, two weeks after returning from Israel/Palestine. Unless otherwise indicated, all these following sermons were spoken at Christ the Lord, a small but growing mission church near San Francisco.

531 villages in 1948 and the expulsion and scattering of their people.

The venue for our learning would be a week-long international conference in Nazareth and Jerusalem sponsored by *Sabeel* - The Way - an ecumenical Christian liberation theology center run by Naim Ateek, an Episcopal priest. The line-up of speakers - 15 Muslim, 13 Jewish and 21 Christians - was impressive and we learned a lot.

There is, however, no substitute for first-hand experience. And mine these past weeks in Palestine has proven to be life-changing. I was stunned, heart-broken, and horrified by what I saw. I still am…and fear I will have a lot to process this Advent.

We travelled the length of the West Bank and to the shuttered gates of a starving Gaza. We visited big cities like Nablus, Ramallah, Bethlehem, Hebron, and Jericho; squalid refugee camps like Aida, Abour, Daheisheh, and Balata; and two tiny villages I will never forget.

In all these places, the *Nakba* - the Catastrophe - is not history. It is an on-going moral outrage and a story that is unknown in this country.

It is a story that, again and again, people begged us to tell - an Episcopal priest in a Galilean village, a Roman Catholic priest in a small West Bank town, a young Muslim urban planner in Hebron, university students in Nablus, and international aid workers refused entry to Gaza.

I promised them I would, so let me start. Perhaps we can talk more at coffee hour or at some later forum, but allow me here to mention just a few things that I found truly morally outrageous. As Israeli Prime Minister Ehud Olmert has recently said: "The time has come to say these things."

Let me start with the Wall - far higher, far uglier than the Berlin Wall I once lived with for two years - a Wall that separates farmers from their fields, workers from their jobs, patients from their medical care.

Then there are the network of Israeli-only roads and checkpoints that have penned the Palestinians into ever smaller, economically unviable Bantustans. The checkpoints are especially humiliating. For example, on one drive from Nablus to Jericho - a distance of maybe forty miles - we had to wait for hours at six checkpoints. It became an all-night affair.

Then there are the Israeli settlements - all illegal under international law, all very permanent - that form an unbroken white line along the hilltops from Hebron to Jerusalem. Several especially large ones surround Bethlehem and East Jerusalem, prevent the natural expansion of those Palestinian communities. From my window in our hotel adjoining Bethlehem's Church of the Nativity, the brightly lit settlement of Har Homa loomed over the Shepherd's Field like some intrusion from Star Wars.

The refugee camps and their children proved particularly hard to bear. At Aida Camp near Bethlehem some 10,000 souls struggle to survive in one half sq. km. At Balata just outside Nablus, 25,000 are crammed into one sq. km. - this, sixty years after the destruction of their villages. The streets - mere alleys - are only an arms' span wide - impassable except on foot. No sunlight gets in the few small windows and those inside look out at gray concrete walls. Hardly a breeding ground for hope.

In old town Nablus and Hebron the situation is nearly as bad. In Hebron, the city center, taken over by extremist settlers, has become a ghost town. One has to pass through a pedestrian checkpoint to gain entry to Abraham's tomb, now a mosque. We had hoped to pray there. After walking through a rotary gate and a metal detector, however, our group was turned back by soldiers of the Israeli Defense Force - or IDF - for no apparent reason. Strolling instead through the now near deserted market, we found it covered by chicken wire...littered with dead animals and garbage tossed from the windows of settler apartments overhead.

Up in Nablus, we walked through a section of the old town that had been besieged for months at a time and that was still subject to nightly raids by the IDF. There were several bombed out or bulldozed houses and, on nearly every corner, their was a makeshift memorial to one or another "martyr" - "Heroes," my young guide from An Najah University whispered. Maybe they were, defending, as they were, their homes and alleyways.

It was at An Najah, I must add, that I experienced the brightest ray of hope on the whole trip. Our student guides from the Zajel Youth Exchange

Program were bright and optimistic and, as we mingled with the more than 10,000 students on two sparkling campuses, we experienced no animosity - only curiosity and a desire to be in touch with the rest of the world. *Zajel*, by the way, means "carrier pigeon," a means of communication, a symbol of peace.

And, now, those villages...in the far southeast corner of the West Bank where the Hebron Hills begin yielding to the desert of the Negev. The first was a Bedouin settlement, Az-Zuweidin, a collection of tents and corrugated metal shacks on the outskirts of the much more substantial Israeli settlement of Karmel. While the expansion of Karmel continues unabated, the IDF, just the week before, had demolished one of the Bedouin shacks. Walking through the rubble, a shiny object caught my eye. I reached down and held it in my hand - a tiny yellow bear once part of some larger toy. It remains my dearest souvenir of Palestine.

A little further down we came to At-Tuwani, a collection of stone hovels on a rock strewn hillside where some 150 people eke out a subsistence living from a small olive grove and as shepherds. Lying in the shadow of the forested Israeli settlement of Ma'on, it has but four substantial buildings - a half-finished well, a clinic, a tiny mosque, and a school attended by eighty children from At-Tuwani and two neighboring villages. With the exception of the school, all those structures are under current demolition orders. The mayor's home had already been demolished and his family now lives in a tent.

Living among the villagers are a few "Internationals" - members of a Christian Peacemaker Team or CPT who accompany shepherds in the fields and escort school children on their daily three hour walks to school from the neighboring villages. It's hard to believe, but those children are attacked most every day by stone-throwing settlers.

As we walked the dusty path toward the school, two carloads of settlers barreled through the village in a cloud of dust. I made little of it at the time, but remembered it well two days later, when I learned that twenty settlers from Ma'on had just attacked a shepherd and a CPT member, killing a donkey, scattering the flock, and injuring the CPT member. All I could think of at the time was "What kind of God do these people believe in?"

I tell you these things not because I believe Palestinians are better than Israeli Jews - or any worse - but just to let you know that there is a Palestinian people and that they are suffering.

You should know also that, in Israel, there are many good Jews who are speaking truth to power, resisting the occupation, and exhibiting great moral courage. I met several and found in them a great source of hope.

Most poignant of all was Josef Ben-Eliezer, an aging veteran of the Palmach. As a teen-ager in 1948, he had participated in the expulsion of Palestinians from Lydda. And, last month, he journeyed to Nazareth from London to tell the story of that horrific event and to ask, toward the end of his life, for forgiveness. I will never forget the breaking of the hushed silence, as Samia Khoury, a member of the Sabeel board, strode to the front of the room and, standing before Josef - as I'm standing before you - said simply "Josef, I forgive you."

And that's what it's all about - truth and reconciliation.

So, what can we here in the Bay Area contribute to that process? Simple, really. As individuals and as a church community, we can:

- promote truth-telling about Palestine and afford the Palestinian people the dignity that comes with the recognition of their humanity;
- support the courageous efforts of the many Israeli and American Jews who seek honest reconciliation;
- urge our church and government to divest from those companies that enable occupation and oppression in the Holy Land;
- urge the new Administration in Washington - as a first priority and at the highest level - to re-engage in the peace process and to bring it to a just and speedy conclusion; and, yes,
- pray.

Pray and, in the spirit of Advent, *wait*...remembering that we are called to wait not just patiently, but positively, optimistically, and, as Henry Nouwen has said, *actively*. There is nothing passive in his mind about Christian waiting. "Those who are waiting," he writes, "are waiting very actively. They know that what they are waiting for is growing from the ground on which they are standing. That's the secret. The secret of waiting is the faith that the seed has been planted, that something has begun." [31]

So, as we await the coming again of the Prince of Peace, let us plant this seed of peace and nurture it in our hearts and in the world, confident that God's peace will reign once more in Jerusalem and throughout Judea. And, when it does, the people will cry: Get you up to a high mountain, O Zion, herald of good tidings; lift up your voice with strength, O Jerusalem, herald of good tidings, lift it up, fear not; say to the cities of Judah, 'Behold your God!'"

AMDG

MOVED WITH ANGER
A SERMON FOR EPIPHANY SIX 2009

Moved with pity, Jesus stretched out his hand and touched him, and said to him, 'I do choose. Be made clean!'[32]

The other day someone asked me what we do with the San Francisco Night Ministry. "What can you do for the homeless on the streets of San Francisco at two o'clock in the morning?" she asked. "Have you converted any of them?"

"I don't know," I replied, "we're simply a ministry of presence, one human being interacting with another on some cold pavement." What can we do? What do we do? We look the people we encounter in the eye to say, simply, without words, "I see you. I respect you, and I love you as another human being." We listen. We talk with each other as equals. And, yes, we touch each other.

You can't imagine how important, how healing it is to physically feel the touch of another human being unless you've lived alone…like those I've met on the street…or, these last nine years, myself.

I especially remember one such encounter one especially cold night a year ago. It was around midnight at the corner of Sutter and Van Ness…a voice crying from a doorway "Help me, Help me, it's too cold tonight. I've got to find a shelter bed." I stopped and looked and saw a man probably younger than me, but looking so much older, his clothes torn, his hair disheveled, a blanket over his shoulders, his hands, outstretched from beneath the blanket, covered with grime and calluses. Our eyes met and he said, in now quiet desperation, "Please help me. I'm a Vietnam veteran."

Without thinking, I asked "Where?" "Danang '67," he replied. Again, without thinking, I replied "Mekong Delta '65." Without another word, we hugged...for a long time.

It was an encounter I hadn't thought much about this past year...not until last week when I started thinking about Jesus' encounter with that leper in Galilee. I started thinking about the loneliness of the leper and about Jesus' reaction. And I started thinking, too, about the stifling formalisms of religion - our own included - that declare some people unclean and, therefore, to be excluded and others worthy of inclusion and love. And I started thinking about, over the centuries, the church has cleaned up and watered down this story.

My mind wandered...to India's "untouchables" and Mother Theresa, to a visit to Kalaupapa on Molokai'i's north coast where aging victims of what we now call Hanson's Disease still live in isolation, to the now shrine-like AIDS ward at San Francisco General, and to all the people the church has kept at arms length over the centuries and in our own lifetimes.

And my thoughts kept coming back to Mark's story...because it's not only central to the ministry of Jesus, but also represents a turning point in that ministry.

Central? I think we all get that part. For Jesus' encounter with the leper comes in the middle of Mark's stories about the many healings Jesus performed in Galilee - healings that thrust him into prominence and, more importantly, that provided proof to the Galileans of his time - and to us - that *this* is no ordinary man.

And leprosy is no ordinary disease. In Jesus' time, it devastated the individual unfortunate enough to contract it...who not only had to struggle with the physical ravages of the disease, but had to do so in enforced isolation and incredible loneliness. And it terrified others in the community. Lepers had to be kept at far more than arm's length. Listen to the strict requirements of the Law in Leviticus:

> The person who has the leprous disease shall wear torn
> clothes and let the hair of his head be disheveled; and he

shall cover his upper lip and cry out, "Unclean, unclean."
He shall remain unclean as long as he has the disease; he
is unclean. He shall live alone; his dwelling shall be
outside the camp.[33]

No, leprosy was not ordinary. And neither was its healing. Indeed, the last previous healing of leprosy reported in the Bible occurred 800 years earlier - the healing we heard about today of that Syrian ingrate Naaman. No, what Jesus did here in terms of healing was truly extraordinary.

Out of desperation, the leper ignored the requirements of Levitcus, drawing ever closer to Jesus, crawling, begging on his knees. And Jesus stretched out his hand…and touched him.

And, by stretching out *his* hand and touching the Galilean leper, Jesus, too, broke the Law of Leviticus. Despite his admonition to silence, this was an act that would surely come to the attention of the priests in Jerusalem, the guardians of the Law. Only *they* could declare someone free of leprosy. It was a process, moreover, that required elaborate formalities.

And herein lies the turning point in the larger story of Jesus' life and ministry. For, by defying the rules of Leviticus and the formalities of the priests, he broke barriers and posed a challenge to all the powers that be in this world.

But, as Obery Hendricks puts it in his *Politics of Jesus*, biblical translators have too often "softened the meaning of words and phrases they thought too challenging to the powers that be."[34] As evidence, he cites the word "tyrant" which appears more than 400 times in the Geneva Bible, an English translation of 1560, but not once in the King James Version fifty years later. One has to wonder, might that have something to do with James' desire to scrub the Bible of ammunition that might be used against him?

In similar fashion, "justice," a communal value, too often gets watered down to "righteousness," an attribute of personal piety…systemic "oppression" becomes personalized "tribulation" and, as Hendricks puts it, "the gaze of the disprivileged masses [is] focused upon personal morality, rather than upon the realization of the holistic justice of God that frees the oppressed and topples tyrants."[35] Put another way, it clouds our vision of the Kingdom of God…that Kingdom of God we would will into existence, when, in a few minutes, we pray that prayer that Jesus taught us: "Thy kingdom come, thy will be done *on Earth* as it is in heaven."

So, how has such wordsmithing softened the meaning of Mark's story? What might be done to heighten its power…to sharpen the point on which ministry of Jesus is about to pivot…from local healer to national celebrity - to Jesus Christ Superstar - whose powerful, provocative message would challenge the powers that be…in his time…and in ours?

Bruce Metzger, a prominent New Testament scholar, focuses on three words, three phrases. In his translation, "pity" - as in "moved with pity" - becomes "anger;" the "sternly warning him" of today's version becomes "snorting with anger;" and, at the end, "a testimony to them" - the priests - becomes "a testimony *against* them." The leper, now healed, shows up at the temple and says, in effect, "See, I didn't need you. Jesus did this, and he didn't need you either!"

Small changes, to be sure, and they don't change the meaning of the story - Jesus the local healer becomes Jesus the breaker of barriers, intent on confronting the priestly class and all that they stand for. Small changes, but they emphasize the barrier-breaking power, authority, and divinity of Christ our Lord…and, at the same time, the *humanity* of Jesus our brother.

And it is from the courageous humanity of Jesus that we draw hope that we might succeed in our own ministry, as we seek to build God's Kingdom "on earth as it is in heaven"…as we seek to fulfill our Baptismal vows…among them to "strive for justice and peace among all people and respect the dignity of every human being."

Dignity! It was, I suspect, the *lack* of dignity that society afforded the crawling, begging Galilean leper that provoked Jesus to "snorting anger."

Confronted by similar situations on the streets of San Francisco, I've always found "pity" much too weak a word, an all too condescending attitude, an unworthy emotion, an inadequate response to what I see as a systemic failure - the failure of our society and government to care for the weakest among us. No, I usually respond - to myself and to God - with anger at how we as a community have failed to "respect the dignity of every human being."

I used to feel guilty about that. Not any more! I've come to the conclusion that sometimes it's okay to be angry. *Jesus* was sometimes angry. Listen to what Hendricks has to say about Jesus and the leper:

> Jesus' response shows us that there are things we should be angry about, there are things we must say and do as a testimony against every action, system, policy, and institution that excludes any of God's children from the fullest fruits of life for any reason. That is to say, we must endeavor to love everyone, but we must also take sides. We cannot be against injustice if we do not take the side of justice. We must be angered by the mistreatment of any of God's children. When we see people hurt and excluded in the name of God, we should be angry.[36]

But anger is not enough. It can motivate, but it cannot achieve. For *that*, we must have hope…a clear vision of what we're striving for - God's Kingdom "on earth as it is in heaven." But can we hold both anger and hope? Mair Honan, another street minister, believes we not only *can*, but that we *must*. Here is what she has to say:

> It seems to be an authentic human need to experience both. If one doesn't feel outrage at the injustice we see and experience we have numbed ourselves to evil, detached ourselves from our connectedness. But, if we don't experience the reality of hope as well, a vision of what can be, we have no compass. Anger cannot be our only motivator. We will only burn. And hope, without the truth that anger reveals, can lead to a contorted Pollyanna response to the human experience. They seem to be like two tracks for the train - we can proceed when hope and

anger are real.[37]

In this story and in his life, Jesus showed us how to proceed. He calls us *all* to be ministers - to "strive for justice and peace among all people and respect the dignity of every human being;" to be angry in the face of injustice, war, and every indignity visited upon our brothers and sisters; and *never* to lose hope that someday - step by step - we will build that Kingdom of God "on earth as it is in heaven."

AMDG

WHAT DOES A DEACON DO?
A SERMON UPON THE INSTALLATION OF A DEACON
TRINITY SUNDAY 2009

And I heard the voice of the Lord saying 'Whom shall I send, and who will go for us?" Then I said, "Here I am! Send me.' [38]

Here I am! You called. I showed up. And, a few moments ago, you took the risky step of declaring it a match. Christ the Lord Church again has a deacon.

I have big shoes to fill, much to live up to. For my predecessors here have been icons of the diaconate. I think especially of Kate Salinaro who I was fortunate to have as a mentor during my formation and am now privileged to call "Friend." In such company, I'm reminded of young Isaiah quaking in the Temple in his inadequacy.

And I hope that, in the future, as you look back on your decision this morning, I don't give you cause to rue it and to exclaim like young Isaiah "Woe is me!"

The calling of a deacon - like the ordination of six new deacons yesterday - offers the opportunity to ruminate on an oft-asked question: "What does a deacon do?" - a question usually followed by "When will you be ordained a priest?" or "Why don't you go all the way."

Well I have gone all the way…at least in terms of ordinations. For I have never felt called to be anything other than a deacon, a vocational deacon. When I learned that that's what Francis was - a deacon, I found that inspiration…and aspiration enough. And, in its fulfillment, I have found just that - fulfillment.

That said, I remain constantly confronted by that question: "What *does* a deacon do?"

The answer is probably best found in the words of examination contained in the rubric for the ordination of a deacon on page 543 of our Book of Common Prayer - words I have internalized and seek to live by. They are words that flash to my lips whenever I hear other deacons muttering about their "prerogatives." Now there's an ugly word - prerogatives. Christians - none of us, not bishops, priests, deacons, senior wardens, or our most newly baptized - have any prerogatives. We are - none of us - here to lord it one over another. We are here among each other to help one another.

For their part, deacons are in the church to empower us all to exercise our shared baptismal ministries. We are not in the church to wear bright sashes, to elevate chalices, or to clutch tightly to some Gospel book, but rather to bring forth what is written on the pages of that Book... "to make Christ and his redemptive love known by…word and example." If anything, we are called to *model* the Gospel, to be icons of sorts of God's love in the world…icons - like Dorothy Day, Martin Luther King, Oscar Romero, and, yes - thank you - Cesar Chavez, none of whom were afraid to get their hands dirty.

In the words of that ordination rubric, we are called "to serve all people, particularly the poor, the weak, the sick, and the lonely" and "to interpret to the church the needs, concerns, and hopes of the world." To do that, we have to get out into the world among God's people and seek in them the face of Jesus. I doubt that any of this is in any diocesan customary, but it's what we need to do if we are to do all that deacons do. And it's what we *all* need to do if we are to do all we're called as to do as Christians.

It is in the duality of this mission that I find the prophetic essence of the calling - diaconal and baptismal - to see and experience the world and to speak about it through the lens of what Rod Dugliss, Dean of the Episcopal School for Deacons, calls the "diaconal hermeneutic."

It is the calling to see the world clearly; to feel its injustice, pain, and violence in one's bones; and to speak truthfully, sometimes painfully, about what we should…and *must* do about it.

It's called being a prophet.

But just what *is* a prophet? And what *is* it about prophets that causes young Isaiah, like all the Biblical prophets, to moan "Woe is Me!"?

Mind you, we're *not* talking about some late night comedian we sometimes knew as Karnak. We're *not* talking about Pat Robertson who talks regularly with God and passes on predictions of earthquakes, tsunamis and terrorist attacks. We're *not* talking about David Koresh who professed to have the key to some Seventh Seal and the knowledge of the time and place of the Second Coming. *Nor* are we talking about those televangelists who nightly warn of Anti-Christs and Armageddon and solicit your "faith offerings."

No, we're talking about people - like Isaiah - called to call their people to do the right thing, to return to the truths they've all known all along and to do what they know in their hearts is required. As Rabbi Abraham Heschel, that preeminent interpreter of ancient prophets, tells us, the "essential task" of *these* prophets "is to declare the word of God to the here and now," and their method is "exhortation not mere prediction."[39]

But, Heschel adds, "The prophet is sent not just to upbraid, but also to strengthen the weak hands and make firm the feeble knees"…to bring "consolation and the hope of reconciliation along with censure and castigation." The prophet, he says, "begins with a message of doom…[and] concludes with a message of hope."

Why, then, are prophets "not acceptable in [their] own country" and, by Heschel's lights, "some of the most disturbing people who ever lived?" The answer, I think, can be found in their often shocking style and, even more, in the nature of their intended audiences - the comfortable and haughty powers-that-be who could if they would - but do not - improve the here and now and who could if they would - but do not - "let justice roll down like waters, and righteousness like a mighty stream (Amos 5:24)."

And that's what it's all about - justice! Prophets understand that the "peace" of *Shalom* is not just the mere absence of war, the quiet of the graveyard. It encompasses rather the justice and positive sense of well-being that underlies true peace. No justice, no peace!

Prophets are hyper-sensitive to the injustices that others may not see or may be willing to ignore…others willing to go along to get along. For prophets, Heschel tells us, "The frankincense of charity fails to sweeten [the] cruelties" of injustice. They are impatient and shrill and iconoclastic. They are not afraid to break the china of cherished certainties in the halls of governmental power or in the sanctuaries of temples.

"To the patriots," Heschel writes, the prophets of Israel "seemed pernicious; to the pious multitude, blasphemous; to the men in authority, seditious." They were, in a few words, embarrassing and dangerous and, therefore, lonely, miserable, and in danger. No wonder Isaiah proclaimed his inadequacy! No wonder Jesus' fellow Nazarenes wanted to throw him off a cliff after being chided by him.

But Jesus and his prophetic predecessors were *right* about the growing gap between their societies' ostentatious moral pretensions and pitiful ethical performance. And they were right *on* the mark in calling attention to the emperor's new clothes…and their priests' old clothes. And, since they were so clearly on the mark, the reaction was often swift and harsh. Witness John the Baptist and Jesus.

End of story? Is *that* all there is? Can we close the book - our Bibles - and say, in detached comfort, "My, that was a good story!"? No, the book's still open and, as our UCC friends remind us, "Never put a period where God has put a comma." No, God is still speaking; revelation is still happening; and prophets are still among us.

In my lifetime alone, we've experienced the words and example, of many prophets. Some, like Dietrich Bonhoeffer, Mohandas Gandhi, Martin Luther King, Jr., and Oscar Romero were, like Jesus and John, killed for their witness. Others, like Walter Rauschenbusch, Dorothy Day, Howard Thurman, Mother Teresa, Henri Nouwen, and William Sloane Coffin died quiet, peaceful deaths…and lived unafraid of death or of censure.

Still others are still living…and still speaking, using words when necessary and always backing up their words with the actions of witness. Some of them are in our Episcopal Church and, I hope, among you.

I think especially of Bishop Marc, who heard others counsel propriety and the dignity of office…and found greater dignity lying on the ground for peace. I think of our Presiding Bishop Katherine, who has urged us to "take our sanctuaries out to the streets to confront the needs of the world." I think of my sister deacon - Diana - who in the dark of night walks the streets of San Francisco encountering Christ in the faces of the homeless. I think of Archbishop Desmond Tutu, who, in speaking truth, brought reconciliation to a troubled people. I think of Sabeel's Naim Ateek, a Palestinian priest who seeks dignity and liberation for his people. And, again, I recall with joy how, last fall, Bonnie Anderson, our lay leader of the Episcopal House of Deputies, reminded us from the pulpit of Grace Cathedral how we are all called by Jesus to be "troublemakers."

As your new deacon, let me echo that call. Go out there and be a troublemaker! Be a prophet! Don't ever be satisfied with this imperfect status quo, with what is. Always keep your eye on what *should* be.

Spread the word! There's a Kingdom to be built. And Jesus needs some willing hands to roll up their sleeves and pick up a hammer.

Spread the word! The message is incredibly powerful, incredibly simple - simple enough to fit on a sign behind home plate. How many times have you seen that guy with the multi-colored afro holding it up at some ballgame? "John 3:16." You heard it again this morning:

> For God so loved the world that he gave his only Son, so that everyone who believes in him may not perish but may have eternal life.

Now, let us all say "*Amen!*"

AMDG

WHO ARE GOD'S SHEEP
A LECTIONARY SERMON FOR EASTER FOUR 2009

I am the good shepherd; I know my own and my own know me….[40a]

Today we hear the voice of the Good Shepherd who, in the words of our Psalm, leads us to green pastures and still waters. How many of us have been comforted by the 23rd Psalm as we've walked through our own valleys of death? And how many before us have been comforted by it…as they took the hand of death and walked without fear to the house of the Lord?

But let's go back to John…and the Good Shepherd Jesus just described and boldly claims to be. Let's talk…not just about the shepherd, but about the sheep...about us.

As in so many of his parables - addressed to listeners in a simple agrarian society - Jesus couches a broader, more profound message in terms a "figure of speech" he says - that farmers, fishermen…and shepherds might understand. Even so, we are told, his listeners here didn't understand his figure of speech. Perhaps because they weren't listening with the open ears of farmers, fishermen, and shepherds. For these were Pharisees - self-important, self-appointed guardians of a frozen orthodoxy. They were refined men - and they ***were*** all men - who were not accustomed to getting their hands dirty or hearing a higher truth from "lesser" men…and certainly not from women.

Had they heard his voice clearly - had they understood - they would have known that, when he railed against the "thieves and bandits" who would break in and lead the sheep astray - as he did in the preceding verse

61

- Jesus was talking not just about the false messiahs then roaming the land, but about the Pharisees themselves - the would-be gatekeepers of the holy.

And, *my*, haven't we had a mighty crowd of gatekeepers in our own lifetimes, those "thieves and bandits' who've seized the keys and even today try to close the gate to those they deem unworthy, arrogating to themselves God's prerogative of separating sheep from goats, of deciding who are God's sheep and, indeed, whether goats are also welcome.

Theirs has always been a shrinking, fearful flock. And, in history - not just in our human time, but God's - they have been confounded, proven wrong again and again, and, ultimately, doomed to failure. For God's welcome - calling us in Jesus' voice, that voice we know - is far bigger than the timid voices of those who have misinterpreted, warped, or not even heard Jesus' message.

Too many Christians read the parable of the Good Shepherd and see in it proof that we - and only we Christians - are to be saved. Didn't Jesus say: "I am the gate. Whoever enters by me will be saved?" Aren't the rest of humanity - all those non-Christians, including God's "Chosen People" - doomed to damnation? So argue all the Pharisees of the world…of Jesus' time and ours. But Jesus shatters their defenses of exclusivity with a bold statement of the radical inclusivity he intends: "I have," he says, "other sheep that do not belong to this fold. I must bring them also, and they will listen to my voice. So there will be one flock, one shepherd."[40b] I don't know about you, but I hear Jesus saying there is but one God and one humanity, intertwined, bound by love, indivisible.

But still there are those who would seek to divide us - from each other and from our God - who see not one humanity, but myriad humans separated into those more or less privileged by gender, race, economic status and all the vicissitudes of birth and life.

For far too long "thieves and bandits" have cherry-picked the Bible to find verses that might justify closing the gates and doors of Christ's church to those not deemed worthy to be members of the flock. And I'm not talking ancient history. I'm talking about our Episcopal Church in the United States of America. I'm talking about events in my lifetime. And I'm talking about events playing out in the church today. The questions are: Who are God's sheep? And who is to decide - God or man?

For the first two centuries of American history - from 1620 to 1865 - from Jamestown to Appomattox - these guardians of the gate resorted to the Bible to justify slavery and, still later, to marginalize African Americans in this, our Episcopal church.

How many of you have heard of Absalom Jones? In 1786, he and another free African American, Richard Allen, were members of St. George's Methodist Episcopal Church in Philadelphia which included both blacks and whites. That year, however, the white members of the church met separately and voted that henceforth black members could only sit in the balcony. Jones and Allen only learned of the decision the following Sunday, when, ushers took them by the shoulders during opening prayers and demanded that they move to the balcony. Jones, Allen, and the other African American parishioners walked out and formed what became St. Thomas African Episcopal Church.

We had gone our separate ways - black and white - and 170 years later Martin Luther King could say - in truth and sadness - "White churchgoers, who insist they are Christians, practice segregation as rigidly in the house of God as they do in movie houses. Too much of the white church is timid and ineffectual, and some of it is shrill in its defense of bigotry and prejudice."[41]

Dr. King also famously said "11:00 o'clock on Sunday morning is the most segregated hour of the week."[42] Half a century later that, unfortunately, is still too often the case.

But it doesn't have to be. Already in the early seventies, for example, I was fortunate enough to find a spiritual home at St. Augustine's in Washington, D.C. where I could worship with Cissy and Thurgood Marshall and, in 1977, welcome John Walker, Washington's first African American bishop, dancing - yes, dancing - down our center aisle in bright robes of kinte cloth.

And it was about that time - barely thirty years ago - that I learned of the "Philadelphia Eleven" - those brave, persistent Episcopal women who had been "irregularly" ordained in 1974. Indeed, I was brought to the Episcopal Church a few years earlier by a young black woman then seeking ordination.

It's hard to believe that that was only thirty-five years ago and that it had taken nearly two thousand years for the church to open this gate for half of Christ's flock.

It's harder still to believe that there are many Anglican bishops, including a few in the United States, who will not ordain women and that in most Anglican provinces women cannot aspire to be bishops.

Just last year, for example, the good priests of Wales voted "No" to accepting women as bishops. Why? Their spokesman reportedly told the BBC that "Christ as God incarnate was male and had chosen only male apostles." Meanwhile, in England, the church reluctantly, barely, consented last year to the ordination of female bishops, but agreed also to appoint alternate bishops to whom male priests, who could not "in good conscience" be obedient to females, might report. And, while we were ecstatic three years ago, when Katherine was chosen our Presiding Bishop, several African bishops have refused to take communion with her. Sometimes one cannot find the humor to mask the pain.

And it is difficult for me as a member of the LGBT community to accept with humor the insults that come our way from so many Christians, "who hate the sin but love the sinner." For *that* is not the voice I hear, when I hear the Good Shepherd calling me to follow.

And following that voice, I found myself identifying last summer with the pain of Bishop Gene Robinson to whom the gate was closed on the eve of Lambeth. Listen to how he expressed that pain to his fellow and sister Episcopal bishops last spring:

> In my most difficult moments, it feels as if, instead of
> leaving the 99 sheep in search of the one, my chief pastor
> and shepherd, the Archbishop of Canterbury, has cut me

out of the herd.

I ask two things of you. Some of you have indicated that if I am not invited, you won't go either. I want to say loud and clear - you must go. You must find your voice. And somehow you have to find my voice and the voices of all the gay and lesbian people in your diocese who, for now, don't have a voice in this setting. I'd much rather be talked to than talked about. But you must go and tell the stories of your people, faithful members of your flock who happen to be lesbian and gay.[43]

Our bishop - Marc - responded not only by attending that every-ten-year conference of the Anglican Communion, but by inviting several of us in our diocese who are gay, lesbian and, yes, transgendered, to join him to tell our stories.

And so I made my pilgrimage to Canterbury…to tell my story and to stand with Bishop Robinson outside the tent, outside the gate.

Imagine then the pain of my transgendered sisters and brothers - who are killed at the rate of one a month by those who hate - when Bishop Robinson decided last fall to make common cause with those in the LGBT community - the Human Rights Campaign and Congressman Barney Frank - who thought it expedient to exclude those most in need of the protections of the Employment Non-Discrimination Act - ENDA - in order to obtain such protections for themselves. "Wait your turn," Mr. Frank told us. And, we were told by the bishop, we who are transgendered must be content, for now, with "half a loaf."

What part of John's Gospel or of today's epistle, I was left wondering, didn't they understand. Might it be "But if any one has the world's goods and sees his brother in need, yet closes his heart against him, how does God's love abide in him?"[44]

It is a question that I and several other transgendered Episcopalians will take to General Convention this summer seeking a full loaf - full inclusion - from our church. Once again, it is time to witness to God's love and to ask that we "not love in word or speech but in deed and in truth."

I'm not sure what that witness might be in its entirety, but my ruminations this week in the quiet of Death Valley have convinced me that it must contain two elements.

First, I must say something about this Good Shepherd who keeps the gate open and who laid down his life that there might be "one flock, one shepherd."

And then I must speak to whomever will listen about a little church in Pinole - a little church with a big heart - where that message is understood and practiced, where the gate is always open, and all are welcome. Where there is room for black and white, yellow, brown, and red; old and young; rich and poor; firm and infirm; straight and gay; and even me.

And, for that, I thank God…and I thank you.

AMDG

JESUS WEPT...AND LAZARUS LAUGHED
A LECTIONARY SERMON FOR LENT FIVE 2010

When Jesus saw her weeping, and the Jews who came with her also weeping, he was greatly disturbed in spirit and deeply moved. He said, 'Where have you laid him?' They said to him, 'Lord, come and see.' Jesus began to weep.[45]

A couple of weeks ago - when it was still raining - Susan and I were driving into The City. Our errands were separate, but both potentially depressing.

Perhaps it was the weather…or our moods, but our conversation turned to death, to grieving, and to how people deal with what some have called our "ultimate concern." To the non-believer, convinced that life is finite and death an end, that ultimate concern can conjure up a fear of death that can warp one's life. To Paul Tillich, the great Christian existentialist, however, our Ultimate Concern is a life-affirming faith in "New Being in Jesus as the Christ," in God as the shared ground of our very being, our eternal being. It is a faith in what Matthew Fox calls the "Cosmic Christ." To Tillich, to Fox, and to me, such faith is a "source of pervasive joy."

Mind you, in my car, in a blinding rain, neither Susan nor I were much interested in an intellectual discussion of comparative theology. We spoke, rather, of the very human reactions to the inevitability of death, and loss, and grief…the sometimes very physical pain observed by C.S. Lewis in *A Grief Observed*, a journal written after the death of Joy, the love of his life. And I, at least, must admit to an interest - more emotional than intellectual - in questions that I'm sure we all share - What lies beyond that veil? Where is the love of *my* life now that she is no longer here? Knowing as I surely do - *in my very bones* - that love does not die, how am I to relate to Mimi now that I can no longer touch her or hear her voice?

To be sure, I've found the hint of an answer in a three-line poem by Mary Oliver written after the death of her partner of over forty years. In that poem, "What I Said at Her Service," she writes: "When we pray to love God perfectly, surely we do not mean *only*." And, she adds - I wish *I* could - "(Lord, see how well I have done.)"[46]

But, still the questions swirl. The very human pain endures. Those questions, that pain…that love, are the very stuff of this Gospel. They are captured in the poetry of John:

> When Jesus saw her weeping, and the Jews who came
> with her also weeping, he was greatly disturbed in spirit
> and deeply moved. He said, "Where have you laid him?"
> They said to him, "Lord, come and see." Jesus began to
> weep.[47]

Here is a profound love, a profound sense of loss that we can all relate to. Jesus, our very human brother "was greatly disturbed in spirit and deeply moved." He "began to weep." Jesus wept because he loved Lazarus…and Martha and Mary.

But, John, the unsentimental theologian, has still other purposes in mind…other reasons for including this story in his Gospel…and for including it here, this Sunday before Palm Sunday, on the eve of the passion of Christ, and Jesus' own death.

First, this raising of Lazarus is, as our Oxford annotation tells us, the "crowning miracle or 'sign' that…reveals Jesus as the giver of life." John, "the disciple who is testifying to these things…has written them down" so that we, who were not there, might believe. And what earnest of belief could be greater, more convincing than the raising of the dead.

And, what could be more provocative! John wants us to know that this crowning, culminating miracle - even more than the driving out of the money changers - was the precipitate cause of Jesus' own death. Listen to the next verses of John, verses you will not hear as we near Holy Week, in part, as Susan said last week, because they can be heard as anti-Semitic by undiscerning ears:

> So the chief priests and the Pharisees gathered the Council and said, "What are we to do? For this man performs many signs. If we let him go on like this, everyone will believe in him, and the Romans will come and take away both our place and our nation." But one of them, Caiaphas, who was high priest that year, said to them, "You know nothing at all. Nor do you understand that it is better for you that one man should die for the people, not that the whole nation should perish"….So from that day on they made plans to put him to death.[48]

Finally - by its placement at the end of Jesus' ministry, on the eve of that planned death - John intends that this story underscore - point to - the triumphal importance of the Resurrection to come.

But let me return to the more immediate and very human story of Lazarus, of Martha and Mary, and of Jesus "who began to weep"…and why, this morning, I find it so hard to relate this story without weeping myself.

Day before yesterday - eleven years ago - it would have been *yesterday* eleven years ago…about four of a sunny afternoon - my Mimi died. I held her hand as she did…and urged her to take the hand on the other side - Jesus'. She did and she smiled.

And, let me tell you about the last time I preached on Lazarus. It, too, remains a painful memory. By way of preface, you know how I also love my dog - Cocoa… out at the front door, an unofficial greeter of sorts. Well, five years ago, I had another dog, another terrier, the Tibetan kind, you know, big flappy ears. Her name was Salsa. That November morning, I was preaching on Lazarus…and she was dying. I couldn't leave her home to die alone. So for the first time - the last time - I took her to church with me…to St. James. I laid her on a blanket, in the sun, in a downstairs classroom…and went upstairs to preach on Lazarus. That afternoon, I took her to an emergency clinic and said "Goodbye."

And, there have been other more recent deaths, deaths this week, that moved me deeply and still have me on the edge of tears - deaths our hate has spawned - Juliano, a peacemaker, a bridge-builder I met in Jenin, who I was just learning to call "friend;" Ronan, a Catholic policeman in Protestant Omagh where so many Grays, Catholic *and* Protestant, still live; those peacemakers in Afghanistan, buried this week under that United Nations flag of peace, because some "Christian" minister burned a holy book and some "Muslim" clerics preached murder as the proper response. And their killers - all of them - will tell you that they killed in the name of religion, in the name of God. But, in doing so, they gave God a bad name. To their sins of hate and murder, they added blasphemy. And, I have to believe, that, once again, Jesus began to weep.

But, midst all the hate and death, midst all the tears - God's included - we're called as Christians to seek the hope embedded in this story, to wrestle with its questions.

Ever wonder what happened to Lazarus…*after* he was raised from the dead? Ever wonder what he experienced on the other side? Remember, his was not a near death experience on some operating table. No, Martha tells Jesus, "already there is a stench because he has been dead four days."

Remember, too, how our story leaves us hanging…how it leaves Lazarus standing there - probably dumbfounded. "Lazarus, come out!" Jesus calls. And

> The dead man came out, his hands and feet bound with
> strips of cloth, and his face wrapped in a cloth. Jesus said
> to them, 'Unbind him, and let him go.[49]

We have to assume that they did, indeed, unbind him and let him go. Then what? Where did he go? What did he do with the rest of his interrupted life? With his next life? What did he remember of his last life - the one with God? And what did he tell people about that experience that they surely must have asked him about? Did he stand there, rubbing his eyes, thinking "Oh, no, not again?"

We're not the first persons to ask such questions. Eugene O'Neill, the Nobel laureate playwright did. And he wrote a play about it. It's called "Lazarus Laughed."

Yes, Jesus wept...and Lazarus laughed. For *this* Lazarus - O'Neill's Lazarus - had experienced that ground of being that is God and returned with the faith in it - in his case, the sure knowledge of it - that is the "source of pervasive joy." He remembered it and laughed.

It is the role of religion - like Lazarus in O'Neill's play - to help us remember something profound, something we have too often forgotten. And, forgetting, we succumb to a culture of death; a life of long, slow dying; and paralyzing fear.

In the play, Lazarus' laughing reaffirmation of life is a threat to the culture of death that is Rome and the Caesars who condemn others to death and, who, as we learn, fear their own. Lazarus is brought to Rome. He stands before Tiberius - a *pitiful* Tiberius who confesses that fear:

> I fear the long nights now in which I lie awake and listen
> to Death dancing around me in the darkness, prancing to
> the drum beat of my heart! And I am afraid, Lazarus -
> afraid there is no sleep beyond there, either![50]

How different the message of Lazarus, the light of God - of life - shining through his laughing eyes. He stands before the chanting crowd. "What is beyond there?" they shout, "What is beyond?" He answers, as O'Neill instructs his actor, "in a voice of loving exultation:"

> There is only life! I heard the heart of Jesus laughing in
> my heart; "There is Eternal life in No," it said, "and there
> is the same Eternal Life in Yes! Death is the fear between."
> And my heart reborn to love of life cried "Yes!" and I
> laughed in the laughter of God...Laugh! Laugh with me!
> Death is dead! Fear is no more! There is only life! There
> is only laughter![51]

And the crowd chants exultingly:

> Laugh! Laugh!
> Laugh with Lazarus!
> Fear is no more!
> There is no death!
> There is only life![52]

We have known this from the womb, we just forgot: There *is* life before life…and after it. There is no end to life…and no beginning. It *is*. God *is*. And - if we remember - that light that is God, that light that is life will shine through us…and we too will be able to laugh…and shout "Life is good… it always was…it always will be."

> Laugh! Laugh!
> There is only life!
> There is only laughter!
> Fear is no more!
> Death is dead![53]

That is the message of Lazarus. *That* is the message of Easter that soon will dawn again - an eternally recurring assurance of life eternal. My prayer for you - for all of us - is simple…that we not forget…that we remember...and laugh.

AMDG

WILL THE REAL JESUS PLEASE STAND UP? A SERMON FOR EASTER TWO HOLOCAUST REMEMBRANCE DAY 2010

Now Jesus did many other signs in the presence of his disciples, which are not written in this book. But these are written so that you may come to believe that Jesus is the Messiah, the Son of God, and that through believing you may have life in his name.[54]

With these words, John ends his Gospel and states his purpose in writing it. Ah, but you say, there's another chapter. Yes, but it's only an epilogue…written later by someone else.

With these words, John has completed his work and, together, the four Gospel writers have completed theirs.

They have laid before us all the words of Jesus, all the stories of his signs and miracles, all the evidence that "Jesus is the Messiah, the Son of God," so that we may "come to believe…and that through believing [we] may have life in his name."[55]

Are these words enough? Do we believe? Do we *really* believe? Is this second-hand evidence enough…or must we, like Thomas, physically stick our fingers through the holes in his wrists…or plunge our hands into the gaping wound in his side, before we, like Thomas, can kneel before Jesus and repeat that profoundest of testimonies - "My Lord and my God."

We've waved our palm fronds, we've shouted our alleluias on Easter morning. What do we do now? Pack it away for another year…content that we've done our "annual duty," gone through the obligatory motions? Or is there more to all this…this Resurrection, this walking through locked doors, this Messiah we're asked to believe in.

In the wake of our Holy Week and all this Good News about Jesus, I ask you to pause this Easter season and ponder, in all seriousness, what you really believe about Jesus.

It is a question that demands our attention more than ever. For, this year, in this country, false prophets - folks like Glenn Beck - are asking us to believe in a Jesus I just cannot recognize in the written evidence presented by John and the other Evangelists or in the one-on-one encounters of my prayer life. Beck's Jesus is a selfish, worldly, solitary Jesus who would turn his back on the poor, on community, on solidarity, on justice.

In times like these, we have to ask "Will the *real* Jesus please stand up?!" And *we* have to be prepared to stand up for Jesus - our Lord and our God.

Today's readings…and the calendar…suggest one way that we - as individuals and as a church - can stand up for Jesus. For us it is the first Sunday after Easter. But, in the Holy Land, the calendar reminds us, it is also Holocaust Remembrance Day, *Yom HaSho'ah*…a time to recall in sorrow man's capacity for evil. At noon, the sounds of sirens will mix with those of church bells around Jerusalem. And, as the confusing cacaphony subsides, a now-old cry - "Never again!" - will echo through suddenly silent streets and alleys…leaving us to wonder: What we to make of those words? What are we to do with them?

In *Fatal Embrace*, a book I recommended in the April newsletter, Mark Braverman draws our attention to the Holocaust and to the "parallel crises" that face us in its wake - as Jews and as Christians.[56] The Jewish crisis, he says, is the struggle to untangle the exclusivist narrative of a chosen people from the universal moral/ethical message of the prophets. The Christian crisis entails the struggle to rid the church of millennia of anti-Jewish bias in its teachings.

"What anti-Jewish bias?" you ask. Consider today's Gospel. Why were "the doors of the house where the disciples had met… locked?" They were locked "for fear of the Jews;" not the Romans…the Jews. And why were the Jews to be feared? Consider our reading today from Acts. The Apostles, emboldened by the Holy Spirit, had begun preaching in the name of Jesus around Jerusalem and in the Temple itself. It got them arrested...here a second time. And in his questioning of them, the high priest's voice rises to anger pitch: "We gave you strict orders not to teach in this name, yet here you have filled Jerusalem with your teaching and you are determined to bring this man's blood on us."[57]

That is the infamous "blood libel" that, from the beginning, gave rise to anti-Semitism. It was, we were told again and again, the Jews who killed Christ. His blood was on their hands and, for that, they were to be dispersed and despised for all time.

That libel festered as a darkness in the heart of European Christianity over the centuries. For years, I lived in its shadow...in Munich, just a few miles from Dachau and a few more from Oberammergau, where every Lent John's Passion was played out by hooked-nosed actors shouting "Crucify him! Crucify him!"...and in Krakow, just an hour's drive from Auschwitz where such anti-Semitism culminated in the Holocaust.

The uniqueness of the Holocaust lies not just in the magnitude of the crime, the horror of which has indelibly stamped a sense of insecurity and victimhood on the souls of Jews, but also in the nature of the discontinuity - the break - it represents in the Christian experience of anti-Semitism. The subsequent sense of guilt among Western Christians has been profound.

In neither instance - the fear or the guilt - have the consequences always been healthy. They have given rise to the "parallel crises" that Braverman contends cloud our vision of current realities in the Holy Land and prevent frank discussion of the day-to-day injustices inflicted upon Palestinians there. They are, he adds, crises that must be addressed within our separate traditions - the theme of justice voiced by the prophets and of love embodied by Jesus. That, he says, may take longer for Jews than Christians. But, he adds, "Don't wait for us. You work on your problem. We'll work on ours."[58]

So *what* is our problem in this regard? It is that we have not really addressed - not historically nor theologically - the anti-Judaism in John and

Acts and Paul; it is also how, over the centuries, that failure - that sin of omission - warped into the anti-Semitism that led to the Holocaust.

Since the Holocaust, we have swept the facts of early church history under the rug, preferring instead new theological stratagems designed to stress the continuities between Judaism and Christianity, between the Old Testament and the New - stratagems that, in their guilt-ridden enthusiasm, blur the discontinuities and reduce Jesus to but one in a long list of Jewish prophets. Anti-Semitism has been replaced by fawning philo-Semitism. Jews - and by extension, Israel - can do no wrong.

That, Braverman says, does Jews no favors. Instead, he says, it "thwarts Jewish renewal by insulating us from the painful process of self-reflection about the effects of particularlism and exceptionalism."[59]

And it does Christians no favors. Instead, it enables us to avoid facing and dealing with our real guilt. We have locked the Holocaust in the hermetically sealed box of another time and place. And we have fobbed off the consequences onto another people - the Palestinians - who had nothing to do with the crime.

It didn't happen here. It didn't happen on our watch. We twenty-first-century Californians had nothing to do with it. Like Pilate, we can wash our hands of the whole affair. The Germans did it. And they did it more than sixty years ago.

"Not so fast, not so easy," warns Zygmunt Bauman, a Polish Jew and sociologist. In *Modernity and the Holocaust*, he writes;

> …the exercise in focusing on the *Germaness* of the crime as on that aspect in which the explanation of the crime must lie is simultaneously an exercise in exonerating everyone else, and particularly *everything* else. The implication that the perpetrators of the Holocaust were a wound or a malady of our civilization - rather than its horrifying, yet legitimate product results not only in the moral comfort of self-exculpation, but also in the dire threat of moral and political disarmament. It all happened

'out there' - in another time, another country. The more
'they' are to blame, the more the rest of 'us' are safe, and
the less we have to do to defend this safety.[60]

Those of you who attended the Taize service Good Friday evening may have noticed that there were tears behind my eyes, as we sang "Were You There When They Crucified My Lord." Those tears were there, because I cannot escape the theology of that hymn or the truth of Bauman's wisdom.

It wasn't just the Jews - or the Romans - who killed Jesus. We all did. We were all there.

And it wasn't just the Germans of a certain era who had the capacity to kill six million Jews. In our hearts of darkness, we are all capable of similar crimes. Need I mention the genocide in which millions of Native Americans were killed, the centuries-long crime of slavery, the concentration camps in which we confined our Japanese Americans, or the hatred so many of us harbor for the Muslims in our midst.

Only when we confront the universality of evil and embrace the redemptive theology that proceeds from the resurrected Jesus, will we be able to deal in a healthy way with the guilt that is our Christian Holocaust problem.

And only when we accept that Jesus - the Christ - is far more than just the product of his Jewishness, but rather its fulfillment…the New Adam who represents the break in human history through which the exclusive God of the Jews becomes the God of all…only then will we be able to help Jews deal with *their* Holocaust problem in a healthy way - to break the bonds of exclusivity and to embrace the universality of the one God we all worship.

In that instance, we - all God's children - can say with new understanding, new fervor - "Never Again!" Never again for any of God's children - not Jews…in Israel, not Christians in Darfur or El Salvador, not Buddhists in Cambodia, not Hindus in Mumbai, and not Palestinians, be they Muslims in Gaza or Christians in Bethlehem.

And, in the process, I think we will find the Jesus that John and the other Evangelists are pointing us toward, the Jesus we are looking for, the Jesus we can believe in, the Jesus we can stand up for... the Jesus we can kneel down before and say "My Lord and my God."

AMDG

WHICH SIDE ARE YOU ON?
A LECTIONARY SERMON FOR PENTECOST TWELVE 2010

I came to bring fire to the earth, and how I wish it were already kindled! I have a baptism with which to be baptized, and what stress I am under until it is completed! Do you think that I have come to bring peace to the earth? No, I tell you, but rather division![61]

Wow! How do these words jibe with all those words about peace I've spoken from this pulpit? With all the feel-good words spoken from so many pulpits in so many feel-good churches?

The *New Oxford Annotated Bible* I received at ordination calls these words – Jesus' mission as he describes it here - "controversial." "Controversial? How's that for a cop-out?"

Controversy? Not to worry. We Episcopalians, we Anglicans, we thrive on it. Isn't that what we're all about? Since I joined the church in 1971, ours has been one long, never-ending story of controversy. Would we have a new Prayer Book? Would our Sunday worship be Morning Prayer or the Eucharist? Would our Eucharist be Rite I or Rite II? Would we ordain women? Would we accept gays and lesbians?

But these controversies have all been self-centered, inward looking, focused on our ecclesial navel…on our church structure, on how we'll build our walls, how we'll set the table, how we'll arrange the seats, who will guard our doors, and who we'll let walk through them. They have, moreover, been heated and have consumed an inordinate amount of time and energy. And, in many ways, they have left us distracted and exhausted. Too exhausted, one wonders, for Jesus' controversial mission?

One must also wonder, have we – we Christians – ever owned up to that mission? Have we ever really understood it, embraced it, acted upon it? Really? Do we today "know how to interpret the present time?"

Are *we* – this Episcopal Church, this self-satisfied country, our satiated Christian West – the burnt out case Christ would kindle with new fire? Have we produced sweet fruit for wine…or, like Isaiah's Jerusalem, bitter, inedible wild grapes? Too often, I fear, our grapes have indeed been inedible.

I fear we've lost our way and let the flame burn low. In a process that began nearly 1,700 years ago, when Constantine co-opted the church, taking it to his bosom, making it the official religion of his very worldly empire, the church has, step-by-step, abandoned Christ's message of fire and division, of combat with every earthly empire.

As Walter Wink put it in his *Powers That Be*,

> Once Christianity became the religion of the empire…its success was linked to the success of the empire and preservation of the empire became the decisive criterion for ethical behavior….Because society was now regarded as Christian, atonement became a highly individual transaction between the believer and God. The idea that the work of Christ involves the radical critique of society was largely abandoned.[62]

Worship was transformed from fellowship around simple tables in house churches to regal processions in huge basilicas. The church's leaders crowned and blessed earthly kings and, in Rome, assumed a kingly mantle. Those persecuted in the Coliseum became persecutors. Heretics were hunted down and burned at the stake. Armies were raised and Crusades launched against those who prayed to God in different ways or threatened Rome's power. And, over time, the Gospel was tamed. Its more inconvenient passages – inconvenient to those in power – were re-written or ignored.

Ah, but you say, that's all ancient history. And, anyway, they were all

Roman Catholics. *We're* different.

Oh? How different? How different really is the Anglican Church, our mother Church of England. It was founded after all by a not very savory king and launched its own persecutions, burning Roman Catholics like Thomas More at other stakes. Even today it is England's official church. Its Archbishop of Canterbury is approved by Parliament and confirmed by the Queen who is "Defender of the Faith." And it has been tamed to the point of irrelevance in an England that is largely post-Christian.

For much of its life, our Episcopal Church has also been tamed. For too long we embraced power and were embraced by power. We were, as I've said before, the proud "church of presidents" and CEOs and we modulated Christ's Gospel to accommodate too many men in blue suits.

A good friend of mine was junior warden at a prominent church in Washington, D.C., a church frequented by political movers and shakers. He and his wife left, because the rector would not speak truth to power, face-to-face…would not question the morality of pre-emptive war or "shock and awe," would not raise the concerns of the homeless or the poor.

Unable to take the silence any longer, they wrote me in what they called a "spiritual crisis," asking in anguish and anger "What kind of church is this?!" We talked and I'm happy to say that they've discovered yet another church, another Episcopal Church – like the one I attended when I lived in Washington - where African Americans, women, and gays not only sit in the pews but stand at the altar and where the Gospel is preached in all its discomforting power.

I'm sad to say, however, that those who are discomforted and who lament their waning power are fighting back – in our church, in our nation, and in a suffering world. There *is* conflict. And, yes, there is division. And we are called by Jesus not to paper over the divisions, nor to make nice and feel good. No, we are called to "know how to interpret the present time," to join the fray, to share Christ's stress, to submit to the cleansing baptism of fire in a very partisan struggle for Christ, at his side, until his mission – *our* mission – is completed "on earth as it is in heaven."

This requires distancing ourselves, divorcing ourselves, freeing ourselves, from corrupting power…freeing ourselves to speak truth prophetically to all the powers that be – governments, corporations, and, yes, church hierarchies…freeing ourselves to speak the truth that is Christ's preference for the poor and marginalized, to kindle the smoldering "fire" that is God's zeal for justice…the justice without which there can be no peace.

It has only been in the last century or so that liberated Christians, fired by that zeal, have poked at the embers of a church grown cold. And it began in America, this beloved land where we insist, despite the evidence of history and of our eyes, that "all men are created equal."

Someone who believed that…and that all men are created in the image of God was the Oakland poet and devout Christian Edwin Markham. He believed also the evidence of his eyes – the beast-like existence working men and women had been pummeled to by their fellow men, the robber barons of the Industrial Revolution. Gazing at a painting by Jean Francois Millet, he wrote in 1899 his "Man with a Hoe":

> Bowed by the weight of centuries he leans
> Upon his hoe and gazes on the ground
> The emptiness of ages on his face,
> And on his back the burden of the world.
> Who made him dead to rapture and despair,
> A thing that grieves not and that never
> Hopes
> Stolid and stunned, a brother to the ox?

And, in closing, Markham warned:

> O masters, lords and rulers in all lands
> How will the future reckon with this Man?
> How answer his brute question in that hour
> When whirlwinds of rebellion shake the
> world
> How will it be with kingdoms and with

Kings –
With those who shaped him to the thing he
is –
When this dumb terror shall reply to God
After the silence of the centuries?[63]

And, about the same time, a young Methodist minister also believed the evidence of his eyes - the grinding poverty all around him in "Hell's Kitchen" on Manhattan's lower East Side. And, in 1907, that minister, Walter Rauschenbusch, wrote *Christianity and the Social Crisis*, a book that wrestled with Markham's questions and Jesus' message of today of struggle and zeal for the Kingdom of God. For a century now it has defined what we know as the Social Gospel. In it, Rauschenbusch wrote:

There was a revolutionary consciousness to Jesus….Jesus
knew that he had come to kindle a fire on earth. Much as
he loved peace, he knew that the actual result of his work
would be not peace but the sword….[64]

If, however, there was a revolutionary edge to Jesus' methods, the substance of his message was very much in the mainstream of Jewish prophetic teaching about justice, about God's preference for the poor about his mother's prayer to a God who "has cast down the mighty from their thrones, and lifted up the lowly," and about the inter-related social nature of salvation.

Central to Jesus' message is his hope for the Kingdom of God, which, as Rauschenbusch says, is "not a matter of getting of getting individuals to heaven, but of transforming life on earth into the harmony of heaven." In this task, he adds, "the highest type of goodness is that which puts freely at the service of the community all that man is and can be." Conversely, "the highest type of badness is that which uses up the wealth and happiness and virtue of the community to please self." Seen any of that lately?

Internationally, this message has found voice in the Liberation Theology of the global South, particularly in South and Central America. I think especially of Leonardo Boff of Brazil, of Camillo Torres of

Colombia, of Samuel Ruiz of Chiapas, of Oscar Romero of El Salvador, of Gustavo Gutierrez of Peru, and Dom Helder Camara of Brazil – Dom Helder Camara who famously said "When I give food to the poor they call me a saint. When I ask why the poor have no food they call me a communist."

This is not the place to launch into a treatise on Liberation Theology and I won't. But I will point out that a key element of Liberation Theology is the link it draws between faith and politics.

In addition to being your deacon, I am a political scientist and a politician and from both perspectives – religious and political – I find such a link not only justified, but necessary. For both politics and religion concern themselves with social relationships, how we relate to one another, how we will shape our societies. And good politics, like good religion, seeks to shape a just society.

"Politics," as today's Episcopal Life insert says, "is about the potential of societies to do more, to be more. Politics is about faith. It is about our collective ability to realize the world that Christ advocated for." And, in the words of Leonardo Boff,

> Faith generates commitment to the transformation of society as a way of preparing material for the kingdom here and now – for this kingdom is already beginning, here on earth….And politics is the mighty weapon we have, to build a just society the way God wants.[66]

Thus, good Christians are called to enter the political fray, to feel the heat, to endure the stress…and, where there is division, to take sides. Sometimes, that can be as simple as deciding whom to vote for. Sometimes, it can mean standing up at a meeting of the county supervisors to insist that Conoco-Phillips live up to its obligations to our community to ensure that it does not pollute the air we breathe. Sometimes, it can mean being arrested to draw attention to the plight of immigrants who might be deported if they stood up for their own rights. And, sometimes, it can mean laying down your life for the least among us…and such saints are legion – Dietrich

Bonhoeffer, Mohandas Gandhi, Martin Luther King, Jr., Oscar Romero, Camilo Torres, and Ernesto "Che" Guevara…yes, "Che," who, I discovered in Bolivia, is revered as "San Ernesto" by the miners and peasants for whom he died.

Despite all such efforts, the kingdom will not come easy…not without conflict and struggle. For, as I've said, the powers that be are fighting back.

The Liberation Theologians, who took their inspiration from John XXIII and the Second Vatican Council, have been resisted by a newer - yet older – Vatican, a Vatican which silenced Leonardo Boff, replaced Samuel Ruiz, and disowned Camilo Torres.

Here in America, corporate and political interests that feel threatened by the unvarnished Good News of Jesus Christ have poured millions into financing dissident groups in mainstream Christian churches – Methodists, Presbyterians, Lutherans, and, yes, Episcopalians – ostensibly to combat a "gay agenda" and a lack of scriptural orthodoxy, but, in reality, to silence the Gospel's message of social justice.

And, on our public airwaves, there is a steady drumbeat of fundamentalist nonsense that would have you believe that social justice is some sort of communist plot; that would have you, in the words of Glenn Beck, "run for the doors of any church where the words 'social justice' are uttered." Well, there are the doors. You are in a church – the Episcopal Church – that believes that social justice is the bedrock of the Good News of Jesus Christ.

We are faced with divisions, with conflict, with daily choices. As today's insert tells us "Christ teaches us to work every day for a world that turns to compassion before hate, that chooses wisdom over ignorance, that seeks out hope over despair."

If that's the world you want, you have to choose it and work for it.

It is, says Columbia theologian Walter Brueggemann, "crunch time." "It's time." he says, "to decide, to take sides at some risk, to be with Jesus or against him."[67]

Reminds me of an old union song adapted from an older Baptist hymn

by Florence Reece, a *real* coal miner's daughter:
    Which side are you on, boys
    Which side are you on?"

AMDG

MY CITY OF RUINS
A LECTIONARY SERMON FOR PENTECOST SIXTEEN 2010

I looked, and lo, there was no one at all,
and all the birds of the air had fled.
I looked, and lo, the fruitful land was a desert,
and all its cities were laid in ruins [68]

Today I want to talk about yesterday…and tomorrow. I want to talk about that was done to us on September 11…and about what we're doing to ourselves.

Yesterday, of course, was the ninth anniversary of that awful Tuesday morning. We all know where we were and what we felt. And today is the ninth anniversary of the morning after…when we all "looked, and lo…all the birds of the air had fled." There wasn't a single plane in the sky and the sky and the earth were silent. How very appropriate for a national day of mourning that reminded us all of our private griefs. For a brief and beautiful moment we were all one family in our sorrow.

That Sunday it fell to me to read the Prayers of the People at St. Paul's in Benicia…to try to express the sorrow we all felt. I recalled a dinner Mimi and I had had at Windows on the World atop the South Tower and prayed for all the cooks and waiters who were no more. I prayed for Father Mychal Judge, a Franciscan and chaplain to the firefighters, who died beside them beneath the rubble. I prayed for peace and forgiveness…for those who hated us and for those of us who hate. And, as a New Yorker, I reminded our California congregation that, in this event, we were all New Yorkers.

As a New Yorker, I bore a special pain - to look and see the fruitful land a desert, my city in ruins…and to know that my nineteen-year-old niece, who had been waiting at a bus stop three blocks away, had been enveloped in that awful cloud when the towers fell, and was forced to walk miles to the safety of a cot in some midtown armory.

As a New Yorker and an Episcopalian, I knew too that there was – and is – another St. Paul's…our chapel across the street from the hole that was the North Tower…the clock atop its steeple still stopped at the moment the tower fell. Remembering that moment this week, I recalled a song by Bruce Springsteen. It still reminds me of St. Paul's and my city of ruins:

> There's a blood red circle
> on the cold dark ground
> and the rain is falling down
> The church doors blown open
> I can hear the organ's song
> But the congregation's gone
>
> My city of ruins
> My city of ruins[69]

Six months later – St. Patrick's Day weekend – I visited New York, my niece back again at her lower Manhattan dorm, Ground Zero, and St. Paul's. The dust was still on the tombstones in the graveyard and the chapel was closed except to rescue workers seeking rest and solace and the "deacons in the dust" who sought to serve those who served.

That Saturday night I went to Ground Zero. My niece would not go with me…and, indeed, has still not gone. I stood in silence across the street – mesmerized for hours by the sounds of jackhammers and steam shovels, of trucks carting debris up that block-long ramp; by the slumped bodies and weary faces of policeman, firefighters, and construction workers passing by; by the covered stretcher two of them carried; and, above all, by the lights – the bright white lights pointed down into the hole…and the two blue beams pointed upward, disappearing in the black sky. And in the lights, a never-ending cloud of dust – of ashes I thought – swirled up to that same sky. I couldn't cry, but I did pray.

Next, morning, seeking more formal prayer, I visited Trinity Church, yet another block from that awful hole, for Sunday Eucharist. Nothing special as it started out… "Danny Boy" on a moog synthesizer. It was St. Patrick's Day. And then came the first reading from the Book of the Prophet Ezekiel. It hit me in the heart. I understood the night before in a new way, and, at last, I could cry.

> Then he said to me, 'Prophesy to these bones, and say to them: O dry bones, hear the word of the Lord. Thus says the Lord God to these bones: I will cause breath to enter you, and you shall live. I will lay sinews on you, and will cause flesh to come upon you, and cover you with skin, and put breath in you, and you shall live; and you shall know that I am the Lord….

> Therefore prophesy, and say to them, Thus says the Lord God: I am going to open your graves, and bring you up from your graves, O my people; and I will bring you back to the land of Israel. And you shall know that I am the Lord, when I open your graves, and bring you up from your graves, O my people. I will put my spirit within you, and you shall live…[70]

I could cry too for the way our country had changed since those first days six months earlier. By March, the bombs were already dropping in Afghanistan, our airwaves were inundated with hate speech, and October's time of courage and compassion had been replaced by a season of fear and purple rage.

How I longed for - I still do – those first weeks after September 11 when we came together as a caring family – a shared experience I tried to capture – in the moment – in a short poem I called "October 11:"

> A month's gone by.
> We're not the same
> and no different from all others.

We've found a certain comfort
in discovered vulnerability,
a sharing oneness in our grief,
compassion in the face of fear.

The little flags are everywhere.
But, now, they signal something new,
a loss of hubris,
and new found gravitas,
a sense that, after all these years,
we're finally growing up.

But we didn't grow up. We succumbed to the "great terror" of our Psalm, completing what the terrorists could not complete, replacing common sense with duct tape, lashing out at those who had nothing to do with September 11…and, at each other. Worst of all, we failed to ask the tough questions that might have yielded understanding and wisdom – questions still worth asking…like "Why do they hate us?"

In a sense, we had become like the people of Jeremiah's Israel, about whom the Lord said:

For my people are foolish,
they do not know me;
they are stupid children,
they have no understanding.
They are skilled in doing evil,
but do not know how to do good.[71]

For nearly a decade, we *have* been foolish; and we have done far too much evil and not nearly enough good. There is about our current situation a profound sense of loss. We sense, I think, that we've lost something incredibly valuable and that, in so doing, we've lost our way…that we ourselves are lost.

Nine years on, we still grieve something profound that – uncompleted, not fully processed - we put behind us and nearly forgot about – that brief moment in the wake of September 11 when we came together in unity and solidarity, recognizing the pain of each other, seeking to help each other. In that moment, we realized, I think, that we are a good people and we do know how to do good.

How much more valuable is that realization than any sheep or coin we might have lost? What would we give up to find it once again?

In pondering those questions, I've gained some insight into the deep sense of loss that permeates today's Gospel...that leads Jesus to leave the ninety-nine in the wilderness to go search for the one – the one – that is lost...that, to Him, is so infinitely valuable, so infinitely loved.

I have also found great comfort, great hope in this story. If we are indeed lost, how great the comfort, how great the hope to know that Christ is looking for us...and will not give up.

Can we do less, as we search for what we have lost... for what we might have been and yet can be?

Let me turn now to the difficulties that confront us in that search.

Yes, yesterday was September 11. But, beginning at sunset Friday, it was also Eid-al-Fitr, the joyous Muslim holiday marking the end of Ramadan's month of fasting. It is a holiday when large crowds attend mosque in their Friday best, when there are large family feasts – like our Easter or Christmas family get togethers - and, often, fireworks.

But this year there has been a fear surrounding those celebrations – a fear brought about by the juxtaposition this year of Eid and September 11, by the happenstance of the lunar calendar. For, this year, Muslim Americans fear that other Americans might perceive their celebrations as dancing on the graves of the victims of 9/11.

In this, our summer of discontent, Muslim Americans, tolerance and freedom of religion are facing new risks, as the fires of racial and religious enmity are enflamed by those on the right who would invoke hatred and division for short-term gain in the electoral season just begun. It is an unworthy and dangerous game, this morphing of anti-immigrant xenophobia, of racist appeals to white fears, and, now, of anti-Muslim hysteria.

The story-line of this anti-Muslim hysteria was artificially concocted out of whole cloth by one of the most extreme voices in the blogosphere – Pam Geller of Rupert Murdoch's New York Post who launched her "Monster Mosque" campaign in May and is now organizing rallies against what she's labeled the "Ground Zero Mosque."

Her attempt to link all Muslims with the terrorists who attacked us on September 11 - killing nearly three thousand Americans, including dozens of Muslim Americans - and her cruel and cynical manipulation of the emotions of those whose loved ones died that day were quickly injected into the national bloodstream by politicians seeking to use it as another wedge issue. And, since July, these divisive calumnies have been beaten like a tin drum by Murdoch's Fox News.

But these issues of journalistic ethics and political decency pale before the greater task facing us as the hateful hysteria spreads across the land… as mosques are burned in places like Tennessee, as Florida churches organize Qur'an burnings, as protesters in Temecula, California bring dogs to Friday prayer at a local mosque, as people around the country call for banning hijabs and minarets…all in a time when those who would gut the First and Fourteenth Amendments call for "Second Amendment solutions" to our problems.

It is a very dangerous time. It is a time for all Americans – Christians, Jews, those of other religions, and of none – to stand beside our Muslim brothers and sisters in their hour of vulnerability, as Japanese Americans did on September 11, and as Mayor Michael Bloomberg, Manhattan Borough President Scott Stringer, and Manhattan JCC Executive Director Joy Levitt – all Jews - are doing today.

It is a time to recall the words of President Bush spoken just a week after the terrorist attack on the World Trade Center:

> Americans who mistreat Muslims should be ashamed. In our anger and emotion, our fellow Americans must treat each other with respect….

The face of terror is not the true faith of Islam. That's not
what Islam is all about. Islam is peace.[72]

It is time, too, to recall the words of a German pastor, Martin
Niemoeller – to paraphrase, first they came for the communists, then the
trade unionists, then the Jews….I didn't speak…and, when they came for
me, there was no one left to speak.

What better way to honor our shared dead of September 11 than to
make sure that never happens again…not here, not now, not in our name,
not in America.

What better way to honor our Baptismal vow to "strive for justice and
peace among all people and respect the dignity of every human being" than,
next time someone in your presence gives voice to anti-Muslim hatred, you
not nod your head in silent agreement, but rather speak up, speak out in
strong disagreement.

What better way to share Christ's love with our community than, next
time you meet a Muslim, perhaps a young lady in a hijab on the checkout
line at Safeway, Trader Joe's or Lucky, to turn to her with a smile and offer
a simple greeting: "*Salaam aleikum*"… Peace be with you.

And, in her smile…in her *Aleikum salaam* - the peace she returns - I
think we will find what we lost. I think, too, we will also find that once we
were lost, but now we're found.

AMDG

WHAT IS TRUTH?
A SERMON FOR CHRIST THE KING SUNDAY 2010

Pilate said to him, 'What is truth?'[73]

We made it! To the end of the never-ending Pentecost season. It's Christ the King Sunday. Time to put away the green stoles for another season. And it's good to be home, as we begin a new church year and celebrate together this annual feast of Christ the Lord.

In Mexico – where I was these past few weeks - Christ the King Sunday is a big deal. Statues of Christ are paraded in regal robes, and, despite his protest that "my kingdom is not of this world," one can't help but get the impression that many – like the Apostles themselves – would still prefer a very worldly king.

But Jesus came into this world for a very different purpose. He came, he says, "to bear witness to the truth."

Given the power of that claim, I find myself wondering why our lectionary writers chose to omit Pilate's sarcastic retort: "What is truth?" – the actual final line of today's Gospel reading. They are a claim and a question that have echoed through the ages and that have particular relevance in this post-modern era of deconstruction, relativism, and youthful questioning of every verity.

That questioning, that youthful testing of what to accept as truth is not unwarranted, and, as was the case with Jesus, the answer to "What is truth?" can sometimes be life or death. In a song by the same name – What Is Truth? – an older, wiser Johnny Cash puts it this way:

> A little boy of three sittin' on the floor
> Looks up and says, 'Daddy, what is war?'

'Son, that's when people fight and die.'
The little boy of three says 'Daddy, why?'
A young man of seventeen in Sunday school
Being taught the golden rule.
And by the time another year has gone around
It may be his turn to lay his life down.
Can you blame the voice of youth for asking
'What is truth?'[74]

Einstein, I think, would agree with Cash and that "young man of seventeen." I have in mind the Einstein who wrote: "Unthinking respect for authority is the greatest enemy of truth"[75]…to which I would add: The greatest enemy in the search for truth is the propensity of authority to obfuscate and conceal the inconvenient truth.

No matter how great the barriers, we have an obligation to search for truth. We have an obligation to cut through the obfuscations and concealments that are the half-truths and untruths of our lives, for the search for truth is the search for God. Honestly pursued, that search will reveal something incredibly beautiful and life giving – "the way, the truth, and the life" that is Jesus, that is God. As another holy book, the Qur'an, says so succinctly, "God is truth."

And *that* is "the truth [that] shall make you free." In this sense, it was Jesus – bound and beaten and facing death – who was the free man in this drama played out before the mob on this, the last day of his life. And, paradoxically, it was Pilate, a minor cog in the machinery of a vast empire, who lacked true freedom. As one scholar noted, his "independence is no independence – it is action tightly bound within the confines of a limited and worldly set of controls and inputs….[in which] justice is replaced with deal-making and political expediency." Having been a minor bureaucrat myself, I can say with considerable empathy "Been there. Done that."

Pilate's dilemma – sensing the truth but being forced to deny or at least ignore it – highlights another facet of – a danger in - the search for truth. "The search for truth implies a duty," Einstein says. "One must not conceal any part of what one has recognized to be true."[76] To do so, psychiatrists tell us, leads to cognitive dissonance and, unchecked, risks insanity. Take poor Pontius Pilate whose career landed him in a series of colonial backwaters on the fringes of the Roman Empire – Palestine, Scotland, and, finally, Switzerland where, according to legend, he succumbed to insanity.

In my own career on the fringes of another empire I have witnessed the effects of such cognitive dissonance on other peoples in other places. In Vietnam, I found that a denial of truth led to unsound policies, unnecessary death and destruction…and profound moral anguish. In communist Poland I found a people who saw one reality with their eyes and heard another from their leaders…their lives tormented and shortened by the resultant rage and despair. In Jerusalem last fall, I experienced my own moral outrage at a wall built to pen in an oppressed people on the West Bank, to shield its builders from the truth of the oppression. And, west of that wall, its builders seem oblivious to the fact that, in building their wall, they have walled *themselves* in. They, too, are unfree.

As you know, I just returned from southernmost Mexico where I sought another truth - the reality behind the recent turmoil and simmering tensions in Oaxaca and Chiapas, Mexico's poorest and most diverse states. For the last twenty years, that half of their population who are indigenous Indians have suffered broken promises of land reform; the collapse of their corn economy under the weight of NAFTA – the North American Free Trade Area; the loss of ancestral lands to Mexican cattlemen and American corporations; the suppression of communal self-government; and hundreds of murders at the hands of paramilitary death squads. They are a people fighting desperately against economic and cultural oblivion.

At times that struggle has flared into bloody violence, most notably in 1994 in Chiapas and in 2006 in Oaxaca. For now it has settled into a stand-off of sorts, with the Zapatista rebels controlling about a third of Chiapas and the Popular Assembly of the Peoples of Oaxaca or APPO continuing to operate as an assertive social movement throughout that state. Both groups remain in conversation with the Mexican government and another party to the ongoing *Palabra*, the church.

The details of the current situation are murky and getting at the truth can prove daunting. The complexities are great, indigenous voices have been muffled, the mestizo elites remain in full denial, and the Pilates of the world continue to do their best to obscure the truth from the casual, un-inquisitive tourist. These are all things we can talk about in next week's forum.

But, beyond the pyramids of Palenque, the festivities of the Days of the Dead, and all the bright textiles and other souvenirs, the truth is there for those who seek it.

It is the truth of poverty and injustice that then-Bishop Samuel Ruiz best expressed in a 1993 pastoral letter on the eve of the Zapatista uprising in Chiapas. In that letter – "In This Hour of Grace" – Bishop Sam drew attention to the "poverty…deplorable living conditions…subjugation and exploitation as well as varying degrees of brutality and violation of the dignity of the indigenous" in highland Chiapas. And, in pain and sorrow, he wrote

> If we know that God speaks to us urgently in the cries and
> even the sorrowful silence of those who still do not have
> a voice and sometimes live in desperation, we have to
> know how to read the 'signs of the times,' attending
> carefully to the cries of the poor and the oppressed, of
> those who live on the margins or are tortured, and of all
> those who are persecuted because of race or religion or
> because they have renounced injustice. [77]

That letter, a copy of which was delivered to John Paul II, then in nearby Yucatan, landed Bishop Sam in hot water with the Pope and with the papal nuncio in Mexico City who was gunning for his head.

But it was the truth. Sixteen years later, it remains the truth. It was the truth I found in Chiapas…and in Oaxaca. It is the truth contained in the words of a Zapatista militiaman, a young Mayan: "I want there to be democracy, no more inequality. I am looking for a life worth living, liberation, just like God says."

Just like God says – "And you shall know the truth and the truth shall make you free" – "*La verdad los hara libres.*"

AMDG

WHAT IS CHURCH?
A LECTIONARY SERMON FOR EPIPHANY ONE 2011

He commanded us to preach to the people and to testify that he is the one ordained by God as judge of the living and the dead.[78]

Back when I was in college – in another century…and half a century ago – we had a name for this season of chilly days and early nights, this dull time between football and baseball. We called it the "Dark Ages".

But, if you look at a church calendar, it's anything but dark or dull. These last few days, in particular, have been packed with festive events that vie for our attention and speak of endings, beginnings, and of exciting tasks ahead.

Thursday, of course, was the Epiphany, the feast of the Magi, the three wise men who may have travelled from as far away as Central Asia or even China. And today they travel from stage right to center stage…to take their place, at last, at the manger on our altar.

To us the Epiphany is also the twelfth day of Christmas, the end of Christmas. My second-generation European family called it Little Christmas, the day we "took Christmas down" and put the tree out. Mine is sitting on the curb, waiting for the Boy Scouts to begin the recycling process of mulching.

And, next day - Friday this year - was always Christmas itself, again – not the end, but the beginning - for my Orthodox friends who still use an older calendar.

In the very diverse New York, where I grew up, this confluence of holidays was always the occasion of customs that - to this child at least -

were strange and wondrous and joyous. My Puerto Rican friends, for example, received their gifts not on Christmas, but on the Epiphany - *el Dia de los Tres Reyes or, los Tres Magos* – a day of music and merriment. And they received those gifts not from Santa Claus, but from the Three Kings who had brought other gifts to the Christ child. This Three Kings Day, is observed throughout the Hispanic world and is a tradition that is carried on here in California by our Mexican and Central American neighbors.

Next day – Orthodox Christmas – we would gather at the Battery at the southern tip of Manhattan to watch young Greek men in black Speedos dive into the frigid waters of New York Harbor to retrieve a flower-bedecked cross and receive the blessing of a bearded bishop. Ah, the foolish joys of youth!

And, speaking of youth, of beginnings, there is today Matthew's telling of the Baptism of Jesus, coming "down from Galilee to John on the Jordan," to embark on the path – the way of the Lord – that John has prepared…a mission ordained and blessed by our Creator God whose voice thunders from heaven above: "This is my Son, the Beloved, with whom I am well pleased." It is the beginning of Jesus' ministry…and ours.

And, in our reading from Acts, Peter reminds us of the nature of that ministry…our ministry. Jesus, he tells us

> commanded us to preach to the people and to testify that
> he is the one ordained by God as judge of the living and
> the dead.[79]

Jesus did not command us to form an organization, to construct elaborate flow charts, or to erect buildings where, as the anonymous author of today's "Forward Day-by-Day" devotion says, "people have the opportunity amidst seemly surroundings to worship God, to train their children, to enjoy fellowship…." or, he adds, "to serve as a Christian nucleus in a community." "All that," he says, "is good, but it does not come first."

No, first of all, above all, always, we are to preach, to testify, to witness to the Good News of Jesus Christ, using words, as Francis tells us, only if necessary. We are to carry that Good News to all God's people, bringing that Light we spoke about two weeks ago to the darkest corners of God's world – to the alleys off Polk Street, to the parking lot at Home Depot, to our jails, and to all those other places where people are imprisoned by addictions, illness, and loneliness.

All this begs the question "What is church?" Jesus did not come to found a church in the sense of an organization or a building. And God does not have a denomination. We are Christians, but I doubt that Christ is an Episcopalian.

No, Jesus came not to found that kind of church, but to form a community. And his was a community always on the go. There was no time to rest. No place to settle down and build some Crystal Cathedral. There were no walls that could contain it…growing ever larger, picking up new people as it went, and challenging the powers that be to tear down their walls – walls that would – in Jesus' time and ours – keep the unseemly, the undesirable, the unwashed, the downright smelly away from this altar, from the bread we share…and are called to share with all God's people.

On this score, I have to disagree with our devotional writer – for we are *indeed* called to be the Christian nucleus in the larger community that is the Beloved Community. We are called to be the yeast that mixes with that larger community, the yeast that is kneaded into it, that becomes the bread we all seek.

I raise all this, because this is a special day in yet another way. It is – and I'll bet there's no one here who knows this – Anglican Communion Sunday. And what, you're probably thinking, are we supposed to do with that…think happy thoughts about the Archbishop of Canterbury, about Canterbury Cathedral and Lambeth Palace, about that "Defender of the Faith," Elizabeth II? Pray for unity? With whom? With what?

This Anglican Communion Sunday is another occasion that begs us to ask that question "What is church?" It is a question that takes on a particular urgency, given what is happening within the Anglican Communion and in the Episcopal Church.

How many of you have heard of the proposed Anglican Covenant? About what it contains? Or what it would mean for the Episcopal Church? For us?

I trust, however, that most of you are aware of the turmoil that has bubbled up within Church and Communion these last decades over the role of women and homosexuals and the way in which we interpret Scripture. You don't have to look any further than Stockton or Fresno to catch the drift.

Simply put, the Third World majority in the Anglican Communion, many English bishops, and a small minority of Episcopalians have no room in their version of church for gays and lesbians. They would, moreover, keep women "in their place," and insist on the most literal interpretation of Scripture. So-called "Liberals" on the other hand – most notably the majority of our Episcopal Church, the Anglican Church of Canada, and the Episcopal Churches of Scotland and New Zealand – insist that *all* are welcome at this table and that, when we read Scripture, we do so with our heart *and* our mind.

Since the Lambeth Conference of 1998 - that every-ten-year global gathering of the Anglican Communion - the fundamentalist majority in the Communion has been insisting - increasingly vociferously - that the liberals fall in line. They have set about codifying a confessional orthodoxy and building around it protective walls dividing first-class Anglicans from those on the outside who don't sign onto the *Magisterium* thus defined and accord to the Archbishop of Canterbury the "primacy of honour and respect of bishops in the Anglican Communion as first among equals….and as a focus and means of unity."

If this sounds somewhat Roman, somewhat un-Anglican, it should. It is, however, what that "first among equals," Rowan Williams, has insisted since Lambeth 2008 that Episcopalians must sign onto if we are to remain full-fledged members of the Communion.

He awaits our response…and we are in the process of formulating it for consideration at our 2012 General Convention in Indianapolis. I urge you, as that process moves forward, to familiarize yourselves with it and the Covenant. And I hope that here at Christ the Lord we can dig into this more deeply…for it concerns us all.

You should know, however, that, already in 2008, the General Convention deputation of this diocese informed the Executive Committee of the Episcopal Church that we found in the draft Covenant "not a broad and inclusive statement for union, but a particular instrument for the disciplining of one or two members of the communion" and, as such, a "fundamental change in the nature and understanding of Anglicanism." We stated, moreover, that the proposed processes for considering the Covenant are "totally incompatible with the polity of the Episcopal Church."

There is a new draft on the table and the Executive Committee is collecting responses from dioceses with a due date of April 24. I have little doubt that our response will be much the same as in 2008.

What would that mean? It would mean that sometime after 2012, we may find ourselves outside the Anglican Communion, perhaps in some new arrangement with like-minded churches in Scotland, Canada, and New Zealand. We may even find that we have more in common with our Lutheran or UCC neighbors…or with our Methodist friends up the hill than with the distant Church of England. That may prove discomfiting for some. Others may find it liberating. Either way, we are entering a period when we must ask in new ways "What is church?"…who are we, what do we believe, and what are we called to do?

The whole church – in all its denominations – is going through a shaking out and realigning process that – in the end – will allow us all to believe as we pray and to act as we believe. The Spirit is moving among us and something beautiful is emerging.

Let us reaffirm, as we do in the Nicene Creed, our faith in that Spirit, "the Lord, the giver of life, who proceeds from the Father and the Son." Let us reaffirm our belief in "one holy catholic and apostolic Church" – catholic in the small "C" sense of universal…and unified, apostolic in our sense of mission, of ministry. If we do *that* – if we live our ministry by preaching, testifying, witnessing to the life and love of Jesus Christ – it matters not how big our buildings are, how lovely our garments are, or what we call ourselves. If we model ourselves on the life of Christ and share his love with the least of our brothers and sisters, we *will* be big; we will be lovely; we will be called Christians. In the truest sense of the word, we *will be* church.

AMDG

ON RESISTING EVIL
A LECTIONARY SERMON FOR EPIPHANY FIVE 2011

Will you persevere in resisting evil, and, whenever you fall into sin, repent and return to the Lord?[80]

That is the Baptismal vow we'll be considering today. "Heavy stuff," you're probably thinking. "Let's get ready for a downer – fire and brimstone…sackcloth and ashes…and it's not even Lent."

No, it's not Lent…not for another month and half. No, this week marks the Chinese New Year – Tet to our Vietnamese neighbors. Time for a parade. Time for dragon dancers and firecrackers. Time to wish our Chinese neighbors a "Happy New Year" - *Sun ning phai loc!* Time for a hearty "*Gung hay phat choi*" – "May you enjoy prosperity" – and a time to wear red – the color of prosperity.

And this year – the Year of the Rabbit – we're told will be a good one. My Chinese friends assure me – despite the headlines of the past week - that it will be "a placid year, very much welcomed and needed after the ferocious Year of the Tiger." They assure me – despite the deaths in Cairo – that this will be a time, not of war and violence, but a "congenial time in which diplomacy, international relations and politics will be given a front seat again."

Sounds like *Shalom*, doesn't it? A time of peace and justice and a shared sense of well-being.

Sounds like Jubilee, doesn't it? That every-seven-year plowing under of the old. Isn't that just what we want to do with this last horrible decade – plow it under! Might this be that blessed time…to plow, to sow new seeds, to rest from our labor, to build up our strength as those seeds break ground.

Might this be our time of repentance, of renewal, our second chance, our challenge, as a president said week before last, to "win the future?"

Depends. Depends on how we face up to the challenges...how we seize the opportunity...on whether we act or sit back and do nothing.

It is a choice that has everything to do with that Baptismal vow we're asked to reconsider today: "Will you persevere in resisting evil, and, whenever you fall into sin, repent and return to the Lord?"

Let me explain.

We're reminded today – in Gospel, psalm, and prophecy – of God's commandments, of our call to righteousness, and of judgment. In his Sermon on the Mount, probably his most important teaching, Jesus gives us a new understanding of the law he has come to fulfill and of how we are now to understand God's commandments.

Although he tells us that "not one letter, not one stroke of a letter, will pass from the law until all is accomplished," he makes a clear distinction between the legalistic letter of the law and the spirit – the moral compass – he would have us internalize.

We will hear much more about that in next week's readings, but let me jump ahead to hold up one verse that so well illustrates that distinction. Concerning the Torah's requirements for sacrificial offerings, Jesus says: "So when you are offering your gift at the altar, if you remember that your brother or sister has something against you, leave your gift there before the altar and go; first be reconciled to your brother or sister, and then come and offer your gift." *What,* he is asking, is more important? Whether the animal is kosher, the incense sweet...or *whether* there is love that precedes and infuses the ritual?

In this regard, Jesus draws another distinction - between his disciples – Us! – and the scribes and Pharisses who tend to every jot and tittle of ritual and give righteousness the bad name it still has. He tells us they have lost their "saltiness." Their hollow, formalistic version of religion "is no longer good for anything." It should be "thrown out and trampled under foot."[81] *We,* however, are the "salt of the earth."

But what is salt? As any fisherman or butcher knows, it is a preservative. It is also, as any cook would tell you, a flavoring agent that gives zest to what we eat and how we live. And, therein lies another distinction – between standing still and moving forward, between life and death. To *preserve* the status quo is to stand still, to atrophy, and, soon enough to die. Fittingly enough, it was salt – natron – that the ancient Egyptians used to preserve their dead. Those, however, who would move forward on that adventure of discipleship that Susan talked about are indeed the "salt of the earth," full of life, zesty, savoring every minute, flavoring the world around them, moving out, moving forward.

We are, in that other metaphor Jesus uses, the "light of the world"… on a lampstand, on a hill… to show the way to others, to give light to all. Here Jesus draws yet another distinction - between his disciples, standing tall in that "city built on a hill that cannot be hid," and the scribes and Pharisees, those keepers of a flickering flame, a dying religion. They would preserve it by keeping it to themselves, by hiding it under a bushel. And we all know what happens to a flame when you cover it. You smother it. It dies.

No, we are not called to *preserve* the light of Christ by hiding it, covering it. It is a torch that has been passed to us. We are called to hold it high and carry it to new places, to new people.

I'm reminded in this regard of other metaphors, other analogies.

A moment ago, I referred to the President's vision in his State of the Union speech of winning the future. Maybe some of you also remember a Wisconsin congressman's response to that speech. In it, he warned, "We must not let our safety net become a hammock."

Earlier I drew on the Chinese zodiac's upbeat characterization of the Year of the Rabbit. It is, however, not all sweetness and light. There is a potentially dark side to the year. It is, the Chinese zodiac warns

> a time to watch out that we do not become too indulgent.
> The influence of the Rabbit tends to spoil those who like

too much comfort and thus impair their effectiveness and sense of duty.

Elsewhere, the poet Nikos Kazantzakis warns of the danger of lolling about in our happiness – the happiness, the hammock perhaps, of our faith. At one point in his life, he had, he wrote, "more happiness than a young man needs. I was in danger." "In danger of what?" he was asked. "Of one of these two possibilities," he replied:

> ...either I would grow accustomed to this happiness, whereupon it would lose its intensity and all its glory, or I would not grow accustomed to it and would always consider it as great as before, in which case I would be lost completely. I saw a bee drowned in its honey once, and learned my lesson.[82]

To which I would add, "Don't let your religion become your honey... your hammock...or your personal treasure to be hoarded and hidden." No, we are called to live our faith publicly, to share it...to let "our light shine before others, so that they may see your good works and give glory to your Father in heaven."

Let me return, then, once again, to that Baptismal vow: "Will you persevere in resisting evil, and, whenever you fall into sin, repent and return to the Lord?" I'm not an English teacher, but I recognize that– with perhaps one exception - those are all active verbs – to persevere, to resist, to repent, to return. And "evil" and "sin," as used here, are nouns connoting a force to be resisted and a condition to be avoided.

Too many of us stress the sin to be avoided and the old negative cast of the commandments....Thou shalt *not*...fill in the blank. I don't know how many times I was told in the darkness of the confessional booth how I was to avoid the "occasion of sin" – usually a person or place I could not avoid. It was enough to cause me to hide under my bed. If I was going to make it into heaven, I had to *avoid* the world around me...a world so full of such "occasions." It never occurred to me that such a stance – if hovering in fear on one's knees can ever be called a stance – was the worst form of moral cowardice – paralyzing, stultifying, life-draining.

No, that's not what we're called to by this vow or by Jesus. We are called, rather, to be active…to go out into the world and to confront and resist evil. Indeed, to see evil and flee or to stand by silently is the greatest sin of all.

And there is plenty of evil in the world. It is very real. It invades our hearts and prowls our streets. It sows violence and death wherever it is allowed to take root…be it in Cairo's Tahrir Square or Richmond's "Iron Triangle." But it is *not* all-powerful. It *can* be resisted.

In considering the unspeakable evil of the Holocaust, the Polish Jewish sociologist Zygmunt Bauman writes:

> Evil needs neither enthusiastic followers nor an applauding audience - the instinct of self-preservation will do, encouraged by the comforting thought that it is not my turn yet, thank God: by lying low I can still escape.[83]

But, Bauman adds:

> …putting self-preservation above moral duty is in no way predetermined, inevitable, inescapable. One can be pressed to do [evil], but cannot be forced to do it, and thus one cannot really shift the responsibility for doing it onto those who exerted the pressure. It does not matter how many people chose moral duty over the rationality of self-preservation - what does matter is that some did. Evil is not all-powerful. It can be resisted.[84]

Mind you, this is not some abstraction culled from an arcane theological treatise or a moldy catechism. It is as real as this week's headlines and the flesh and blood people behind them. Nick Kristoff was in Tahrir Square Wednesday night when armed thugs attacked unarmed pro-democracy demonstrators. Next day, he wrote in the *New York Times* about two middle-aged sisters he met that night – Amal and Minna. "They had their heads covered in the conservative Muslim style," he wrote, "and they looked timid and frail as thugs surrounded them, jostled them, shouted at them." "...[W]hen I remember this sickening and bloody day," he continued, "I'll conjure not only the brutality that Mr. Mubarak seems to have sponsored but also the courage and grace of those Egyptians who risked their lives as they sought to reclaim their country....Above all, I'll be inspired by those two sisters standing up to Mr. Mubarak's hoodlums. If they, armed only with their principles, can stand up to Mr. Mubarak's thuggery, can't we all do the same?"[85]

Can't we all do the same? Can't we – armed with our principles, with the call to action of this Sermon on the Mount – take a risk for Jesus? Can't we take to heart his positive, action-oriented version of the commandments ...that others might see our light, our good works...and give glory to God? Can't we "rejoice and be glad"...when we are persecuted for righteousness sake and when people revile us and persecute us and utter all kinds of evil against us falsely on his account? Can't we get off our duff and go out there – beyond our doors, beyond our walls - to comfort those who mourn or who are dispirited, to give courage to the meek, to give food and drink to those who hunger and thirst, to show mercy to those who deserve none, to make peace where there is war, and to do so with the pureness of heart that seeks no reward? Can't we "persevere in resisting evil" by beating it back and plowing it under? Can't we take a risk for Jesus? The sin, the real sin, is to risk nothing...to do nothing...in the face of evil.

Oh, we will sin...often..."in thought word and deed, by what we have done," and, most especially, "*by what we have not done.*" Such is the risk of living. Only the dead do not sin.

Yes, from time to time, we will stumble and fall, but God will credit our trying and pick us up. From time to time, we will miss the mark, but God will credit our taking up the bow and give us a new one.

And, when we *do* – miss the mark, stumble, and fall - what must we do to make it right? It's there in our Baptismal vow. We are to "repent and return to the Lord." The word "repent," as I'm sure most of you know, means to turn...to turn from what is evil and to re-turn to the Lord. "When," as that hymn says today, "true simplicity is gained, to bow and to bend we shan't be ashamed, to turn, turn will be our delight…till by turning, turning we come round right."[86]

And, having come round right, what sort of repentance must we offer? What sort of fast does God require of us? The answer is there in that reading from Isaiah. God, Isaiah, tells us, doesn't want our burnt offerings, our quarrelsome fasts, our ostentatious parading about in sackcloth and ashes. No, God tells Isaiah, there is no amount of such fasting that will "make your voice heard on high." There is no amount of repentance or beating of our breasts that will win us heaven.

No, the fast God chooses, the commandments God would have us act on are not so much passively to avoid sin, but actively to confront and resist evil… proactively to do good and, in so doing, build God's Kingdom. The fast God chooses for us is, as Isaiah tells us:

> to loose the bonds of injustice,
> to undo the thongs of the yoke,
> to let the oppressed go free,
> and to break every yoke?
> Is it not to share your bread with the
> hungry,
> and bring the homeless poor
> into your house;
> when you see the naked, to
> cover them,
> and not to hide yourself from your
> own kin?
> Then your light shall break forth like
> the dawn,
> and your healing shall spring
> up quickly….
> Then you shall call, and the LORD

will answer;
you shall cry for help, and he will
say, Here I am.[87]

Do so with joy, with confidence. For, you know what? You are already forgiven. You are already saved. You don't have to earn it. You can't. That's what's so amazing about God's Grace.

That is the good news!

AMDG

"DO NOT HARDEN YOUR HEARTS..." A LECTIONARY SERMON FOR LENT THREE 2011

For forty years I loathed that generation and said, 'They are a people whose hearts go astray, and they do not regard my ways.' Therefore in my anger I swore, 'They shall not enter my rest.'[88]

Today's readings are full of strange-sounding place names – places named Samaria and Sychar and Massah and Meribah; places of cross-cultural encounters, of testing, of quarreling, and, eventually, of reconciliation and salvation; places that we know today as Nablus, maybe Beer'Sheva and Wadi Rum…and, surely, Israel and Palestine.

For me, however, they are no longer strange or distant places. Their people seem as close as those in Hercules, Pinole, or Richmond. They are people I have met…people I have touched and been touched by. I hold them in my heart and care for them just as surely as I care for those of you in this room. And, doing so, I am saddened, because they are suffering. I am saddened even more, because they are suffering at the hands of a people who have suffered themselves…a good people whose hearts have gone astray…a people who – at great peril – seem to have forgotten the Lord's admonition in today's Psalm: "Do not harden your hearts…."[89]

In the unholy Holy Land I have just returned from - in towns like Sychar of our Gospel and in neighboring modern-day colonies or, as the Israelis call them, "settlements" – two peoples are living together cheek-by-jowl and killing each other because of their proximity to one another in one crowded, contested land.

Theirs is a story as old as today's Old Testament reading, in which we find the Jews – the Israelites – in the midst of their exodus from Egypt to the promised land of Canaan. And it is as new as the twentieth-century colonial project – Zionism – that seeks again to dispossess the Canaanites – the Palestinians, who never really left the land. And in their shared story the land has shaped competing meta-narratives that have shaped the very identities of Israelis and Palestinians.

It is a story woven of the Biblical texts we read each Sunday; of a catastrophic history of Holocaust and Nakba, the ongoing Palestinian catastrophe of exile and occupation; and of a sense of place that is often mythic. It has sustained both Jew and Palestinian through tragedy and exile. It is the "Next year in Jerusalem" of the Passover Haggadah. It is the longing of the now deceased Palestinian national poet Mahmoud Darwish, who dreamt of his distant home and, in a poem called "I Belong There," wrote, "And I cry so that a returning cloud might carry my tears."[90]

In the end, however, Palestine and that portion of it we know as Israel is, as Rabbi Nahman once said, "not an idea, it is stones, vegetation, and soil."[91] It is a beautiful but hardscrabble place where today – this morning – people are dying…and living…to possess those stones and vegetation and soil.

As Christians and as Americans, we have for far too long turned a blind eye to objective rights and wrongs on the ground, ignored often manifest injustice, and uncritically sided with one side - Israel - in that contest.

This stems partly from our lack of understanding of the recent history of the Middle East and, in particular, the century-long conflict surrounding Israel/Palestine. Neither have we been well-served by our news media or the purveyors of pop culture who, until very recently, have generally ignored the Palestinian take on events. And - let's be honest - there is also a degree of racism that colors our view of things. We tend to identify with Israel's Jews. They look like us, they talk like us, they are us; for many come from places like Brooklyn and Los Angeles. The Palestinians? Well, you know, they're kind of swarthy; they wear scruffy beards and, head scarves. They're not like us Judeo-Christians. They're all Muslims…

terrorists. They hate us. They're scary.

These are all issues I hope we can tackle somewhere else – perhaps in some future forum about my trip.

There is, however, one aspect of the pro-Israel bias of American Christians that is best addressed from this place – from a pulpit – and that is the theological basis for such a stance.

There is, first, the post-World War II Christian revisionism that has sought to confront and root out the anti-Semitism that grew out of the traditional church teaching of supersessionism. Boiled down to its essentials, supersessionism taught that:

> - God *chose* the Jewish people to prepare for the coming of Christ.

> - After Christ came, the special role of the Jews ended and was taken over – or superseded - by the church, a spiritual, rather than a physical ethical community in which there was neither Jew nor gentile.

> - The Jews, however, rejected Jesus as the Messiah and refused to enter this new spiritual Israel.

> - God, therefore, scattered the Jews all over the earth.

Over time, this almost benign anti-Semitism of displacement and irrelevance became fused with the more virulently hateful charge of deicide – the charge, rooted in the Gospel of John and later church writings, that it was the Jews who killed Christ.

As someone who lived six years in the shadows of Dachau and Auschwitz, I can vouch for the awful consequences of such flawed theology and the continued necessity of combating it. The Holocaust it gave rise to visited profound trauma not just on Jews, physically, but also on the psyche of Christians who perpetrated it or looked the other way.

That, in turn, resulted in a singularly profound and completely justifiable sense of guilt that has, in many ways, become a dual-edged sword.

In a positive theological sense, the church has gained a healthier understanding of the Jewishness of Jesus and the spiritual rootedness of Christianity in Judaism. We have learned to read the Passion of John with new theological insight. No, it was not the Jews – not just the Jews...or Romans – who crucified Jesus. We crucified Jesus – you and I – just as surely as the Jew who shouted "Give us Barabbas!" or the Roman who pounded the nails into the wood.

Our attempt to right past wrongs, however, has also given rise to a strange form of reverse anti-Semitism. This philo-Semitism – or unquestioning love of Jews - theologically blurs the real distinctions between Judaism and Christianity and denigrates the newness of what Christ has wrought. Politically, it has also led in the popular mind to a melding of the Jewish people, the State of Israel, and the extremist right wing government that now rules Israel. And this imagined person-as-entity can do no wrong. Moreover, any criticism of Israeli policies is immediately labeled anti-Semitic.

This is not good...*not* for guilt-ridden Christians inclined again to look the other way – at crimes now against the Palestinians, not for Israelis sensing a green light for otherwise morally unacceptable behavior, nor for Palestinians and American Jews caught in the middle and left to deal with the consequences of such behavior.

In *Fatal Embrace,* Mark Braverman, a Jew, puts it this way:

> Embracing Jewish election may be one way to resolve the Christian problem of anti-Semitism. Ironically, however, the effect of this is to legitimize, indeed boost, Jewish triumphalism, separateness, and tribalism....Ultimately – and this can already be observed in the reaction of the world to the human rights abuses of the Jewish state – this effort leads to an increase in anti-Semitism, by reinforcing and lending support to Jewish exceptionalism and the

behaviors that flow from that attitude and self-image. If Christians really want to help, if they really want to undo the evils of anti-Semitism, they will do what they can to help us overcome this quality, rather than shoring it up.[92]

Far from helping Israel overcome a model that, he says, "has led to helicopter gunships, a separation wall, the siege of Gaza, the flouting of international law, and the hatred, resentment, and mistrust of an increasingly broad sector of humankind,"[93] post-Holocaust philo-Semitism has given rise to a new phenomenon – an Israel right-or-wrong movement called Christian Zionism.

What you might ask is a *Christian* Zionist? Well, Pat Robertson is a Christian Zionist. So, too, are Tim Lehaye and the *Left Behind* crowd. So, too, is my college roommate, a graduate of Tulsa's Oral Roberts University and one of many thousands of followers of The Rev. John Hagee and his CUFI organization – Christians United for Israel.

They operate from the premise that, as God's chosen people, Jews, today, retain a Biblical right to the Promised Land – a promised land that, by their light, encompasses all of historic Palestine…from the Jordan to the Mediterranean.

Theirs is a confused fundamentalist message that rests on God's Covenant with Abram – you know the one you heard last week: "I will make of you a great nation, and I will bless you, and make your name great, so that you will be a blessing."[94] And it proceeds from a mishmash of misinterpretation derived from various end time readings, especially the Book of Daniel. At the risk of over-simplifying, it goes like this:

- Jews remain God's Chosen People under the unending Covenant of Genesis 12.

- The reestablishment of the State of Israel in 1948 has ushered in the End Times.

- The rebuilding of the Temple on Jerusalem's Temple

Mount will, in turn, expedite the Second Coming of the Messiah and the Day of Judgment.

- On this last day, Jews must convert to Christianity to be saved.

Strange as it may seem, the largely secular leaders of Israel are willing to overlook the inconvenience of that last distasteful step, because they understand that Christian Zionists have interpreted God's undertaking in Genesis 12 – "I will bless those who bless you, and the one who curses you, I will curse" – as a requirement for unswerving support for Israel. And *that* is an incredible convenience for Israeli leaders who know they can count on CUFI to deliver a solid Bible Belt congressional bloc and a sure American veto in the United Nations when push comes to shove on such issues as illegal settlements or last summer's attack on the Gaza flotilla.

But is that what God's promise to Abram is all about? Can God's undertakings be reduced to such crass political calculations? And what do today's readings tell us about the nature of those undertakings…and what we are called to do?

Oh, God promised Abram – Abraham – a great nation, fame, a good name – all the prideful stuff that Abraham as avatar for mankind coveted. But to what end? What purpose? Surely, not just to be the big kid on the block. Not just to beat up on others in the neighborhood.

No, a covenant – any covenant – is a two-sided agreement. In this one, God gave Abram a lot. But, God expected and got a lot in return. God's project, according to Leon Kass, was to "enlist man's ambition and pride… to subdue them."[95] God sought here to exploit Abram's pride in order to "subordinate it in service to righteousness and holiness."[96] God sought, Kass writes, "a nation whose greatness is to be grounded in justice and whose institutions are to aspire to holiness;" in other words, a vehicle for educating mankind to a new way of relating to one another and to God. It is in this sense that Jesus says to the Samaritan woman "salvation is from the Jews."[97]

Yes, God expected a lot from Abraham and his seed…and, in the course of history, God would hold their feet to the fire and, whenever they stumbled…as at Massah and Meribah, would convey his displeasure in no uncertain terms. Sick of their quarreling and testing and hard-heartedness in the desert, he fumes in our Psalm:

> For forty years I loathed that generation and said, "They are a people whose hearts go astray, and they do not regard my ways."

> Therefore, in my anger I swore, "They shall not enter my rest."[98]

They would not, God fumes, "enter my rest." They would not enter that land promised to Abraham and, later, to Moses. To be sure, the people - the Israelites – *would* cross the Jordan into Canaan after forty – probably metaphorical - years. But God would make of Moses a scapegoat. Taking on the repeated shortcomings of his people, Moses would die on the eastern shore, never to enter that rest. And, as he bids farewell to his people, he warns them in Deuteronomy "So be careful not to forget the covenant that the Lord your God made with you….For the Lord your God is a devouring fire, a jealous God."[99]

Fast forward – to a hundred years ago – to Jews returning to Canaan – to Palestine…after an absence of nearly two thousand years. Fast forward to 1948, to 1967, to this morning in East Jerusalem or some village east of Ramallah…to an Israeli settler, a covenant in hand, showing up on the doorstep of some Palestinian family, who have lived in their home for generations, and saying "Get out. Your land belongs to me. God promised it to me." How does such a scene, repeated now many thousands of times over, jibe with your understanding of Biblical truth…with your sense of right and wrong? What, as I've asked before, is truth? And, what is right?

Let me be clear about what I understand…what I do and do *not* believe. I do not believe in tribal choseness. I do not believe in such a little God. My God is far too big for such a tiny box. And so is Abraham, the father of two peoples – Jews and Arabs – and of three great religions, and, as I've just said, the avatar for all mankind. In Abraham, God chose mankind – all mankind – male and female, made in God's image.

Nor do I believe in proof-texting the Bible, cherry-picking passages to "prove" that I'm right, that you're wrong, or that God is on my side. God, again, is far too big for such parochial turf wars. And, I certainly don't believe in the validity of Biblical covenants as twenty-first century real estate deeds.

Nor do I believe that the Bible is to be taken as an unerringly literal recitation of history. Particularly with regard to Genesis or Exodus, we are dealing with metaphors…of oral, pre-historic, foundational tales coming to us across the mists of time. That is not to say that such tales are untrue. Indeed, as in these tales of Abraham and Moses, these metaphors – if that's what they are – contain a metaphysical truth that transcends mundane historicity.

Metaphorical or literal, metaphysical or historical, Moses' warning to his people upon their fateful crossing of the Jordan smacks of a truth that they and we must still hear…and heed: "So be careful not to forget the covenant that the Lord your God made with you….For the Lord your God is a devouring fire, a jealous God."[100]

But Israel today – the Israel I experienced just weeks ago – seems to have a defective, very selective memory of that covenant. Its people remember what they were promised – the land, the name, the fame. Puffed up with pride and putting their trust not in God, but in their perceived military prowess, however, they seem to have forgotten the part about justice and righteousness and holiness. Once again, they seem to have hardened their hearts and, now, closed their eyes to the suffering of their Palestinian sisters and brothers.

For far too long the church, too, has turned a blind eye to that suffering. Fearful that we might be labeled anti-Semitic, too many Christians have been reluctant to speak out against the human rights abuses of the Israeli government against the Palestinian people, so many of whom are

Christians. But not to speak out is to be guilty of a greater sin...the sin of silence.

So, let us look...and see...and speak, mindful always of what Abraham's covenant – our covenant – requires of us all, Christians, Jews, and Muslims...and mindful also of what Jesus called us to on a hillside in his now suffering Holy Land:

> Blessed are the peacemakers, for they shall be called children of God.

> Blessed are you when people revile you and persecute you and utter all kinds of evil against you falsely on my account.[101]

AMDG

THE GIFT OF OTHERNESS
A LECTIONARY SERMON FOR PENTECOST TWO 2011

Whoever welcomes you welcomes me, and whoever welcomes me welcomes the one who sent me.[102]

Right about now Bishop Gene Robinson – or some nameless deacon - should be concluding a curbside Eucharist under the Bay Bridge and very soon Bishop Robinson, and the Lutheran's Bishop Mark Holmerud will lead a contingent of Episcopalians and Lutherans down Market Street, bringing up the rear of San Francisco's Pride Parade.

And proud they should be, for, with their feet, they are witnessing to today's Gospel and to what it means to be a Christian. With their outstretched arms and the warmth of their smiles, they are saying to the thousands lining the route: "We welcome you!" And, as someone who has made that march and exchanged high fives and a shouted "God loves you!" with those along the way, I can assure you that the spectators will respond – some with surprise, some with joy, most with love – "*We* welcome *you*!" And the response of many will be tinged with relief. In their faces, I have read that relief…a relief that says with gratitude "We have been waiting for you. We have been waiting for a church with open doors and open hearts, a church that offers a cup of cold water to thirsting newcomers."

This morning – for the first time in years and with some sorrow – I am missing the joy of that experience. And I *do* miss it. But, this morning, *this* Pride morning, I feel a need to be with you…to say "Thank you," to say thank you for welcoming me and other thirsty newcomers. I feel a need also to say "Well done!" Well done, because, in our own quiet way, we are living into Christ's Gospel of radical welcome.

That is no small feat. Once, at another church, I was not so welcomed. All they'd hear from me, it was whispered, would be sermons on sex. Now, I know I've troubled you about any number of troubling issues. Like Bonnie Anderson, I feel Christians are called to be troublemakers. Justice is never achieved in silence. But, I trust you'll agree, I haven't spoken much about sex. And I won't this morning. For I've never felt the need to beat a drum about who I am and whom I love. I've never felt a need to wear an armband, or carry a placard, at least not in church.

By the same token, however, I have not tried to hide – as if I could – who I am. Nor have I tried to hide that Mimi and I were very much in love for thirty-five years…and still are. Paul was right, love *does* not die.

Love, moreover, demands honesty. It holds nothing back and risks everything. It risks rejection.

I came here, at first, tentatively, testing the waters, like many of you dropping in for the occasional service. And, in the process, I found a community I could love…that I wanted to be a part of. But I could not love you fully, if I could not be fully honest with you…if I did not risk your rejection. In saying "I want to be your deacon," I risked a lot…and I challenged *you* to risk a lot.

In a book she co-authored with CDSP's Bill Countryman – *Gifted by Otherness*…a book about coming out in church – the late M.R. Ritley once wrote "How can you be a gift to others, if they don't know you're there."[103] The "otherness" she wrote about was about being gay. It might just as well have been about being black or brown or yellow; about being elderly, disabled, or homeless; or…about being transgendered. And the "gift?" It is the opportunity such "otherness" offers in terms of stretching our spiritual envelopes, the challenge it poses to our willingness to live into Christ's call to be welcoming.

Continuing with M.R.'s theme of openness and honesty – the honesty that love requires – let me be open about the price such a "gift" sometimes requires of the giver. A good gift is never cheap. Even the widow's mite was not cheap.

I came out – Mimi and I came out together – in a quiet, suburban church that had once known us as Vic and Mimi. It was not easy, but we loved the community we found in that church, St. Paul's in Benicia, and we wanted to stay. So we risked the myriad questions and a few harsh words. It took special fortitude – and love – on Mimi's part. As I wrote after the experience,

> You want guts?! Mimi had them, as she walked before me
> to communion on Vicki's first Sunday in church. It was a
> breeze for me, thereafter. Mimi was always there before
> me; I sensed Christ there behind me; and we all smiled
> on the way back. Mimi was there, too, that morning, when
> in our prayer group, someone insisted on speaking his
> mind about my "sin." She held my hand, as I held his, as
> he read from his Bible that I was an "abomination." I will
> never forget the trembling and perspiration of his hand
> and the coolness and firmness of Mimi's.[104]

We took a risk. We paid a price. And, in the end, before she died, we were rewarded. For, in the end, our love was reciprocated. The people of St. Paul's came to love us as much as we loved them. They, too, took a risk. And neither they nor we were ever the same again.

And, therein lies another facet of this welcoming thing – the price the *community* must pay, the reward *it* will reap – both in terms of change. Nothing, we discover, will ever be the same if we truly welcome the stranger, the newcomer, the "other." We cannot say "Welcome, but, sorry, we don't intend to change. You can join us, but we want you to look like us, to be like us, to fit in with us as we are." Oh, the newcomer will change…some. But, if we really mean our welcome, so will the community. Like adding yeast to the dough, together, we will become something entirely new…and wonderful. *That* is the "prophet's reward… .the reward of the righteous."

That is what I reaped at St. Paul's; at Christ Church Alameda, which raised me to ordination; at St. James San Francisco; and here at Christ the Lord. And, that is why, when it came time to be deployed as a deacon, I resisted being assigned to a so-called "gay friendly" church. For I feared that, in such an environment, I would have no gift to give, I would not be challenged. There would be no yeast to bring, no change to reap.

In retrospect, however, there may indeed be a gift I can offer the LGBT community... a gift that has nothing to do with being a member of that community and everything to do with it. It is a message not voiced often enough in our LGBT community - that those of us who are gay, lesbian, or transgendered need not huddle together in self-imposed ghettos...that we can be – must be - part of a larger beloved community in which "there is no longer Jew or Greek, there is no longer slave or free, there is no longer male and female;"[105] where all are one in Jesus Christ...and no one is "Other."

For that to happen, however, requires that those of us in the LGBT community take the risk of breaking down the walls of our physical and spiritual ghettos. I use the word "risk" advisedly, deliberately, for walls can both protect and confine, and ghettos can be both prisons and places of comfort. It can be comfortable – *and* dangerous – to "stick with one's own," be it in the Castro, Richmond, Pinole, or Pacific Heights. And it can be comfortable – *and* dangerous – to focus on one issue, on one's *own* issue, on one's *own* plight, on one's *own* rights, while paying scant attention to the rights of others – immigrants, hotel workers, the homeless, Palestinians, Syrians, so many others. If those of us who are gay or lesbian or transgendered would gain and enjoy *our* rights, guilt free, we must be there for others who seek theirs. There are no rights in isolation. For a Christian, it is not tenable to be a one-issue, one dimensional person in a three-dimensional world, in which so many are suffering.

Those same imperatives also apply here in Pinole...for all of us. If we are to be a truly welcoming community that is part of that larger beloved community in which there is no longer rich or poor, no longer black or white...or brown or red, no longer old or young, no longer firm or infirm, and, yes, no longer straight or gay, then we, too, will have to break down our walls and break out of our ghettos, real and imagined.

We are, I think, learning to do that. We are, if only by osmosis, learning that there are no "others" among us…that we are all God's children made in the same image of that one true God. To paraphrase Shakespeare:

> Have we not all eyes? Have we not all hands,
> organs, dimensions, senses, affections, passions;
> fed with the same food, hurt with the same
> weapons, subject to the same diseases, healed
> by the same means, warmed and cooled by the
> same winter and summer? If you prick us, do we
> not bleed? If you tickle us, do we not laugh? If
> you poison us, do we not die?[106]

And we are coming to the realization that there is nothing special about LGBT rights, women's rights, immigrant's rights…*anyone's* rights. They are all simply human rights. And we must all stand up for the God-given rights of our shared humanity.

Maybe next year I'll march again in that parade on Pride Sunday. Maybe some of you will join me. Maybe, together, we'll demonstrate throughout the year and in the years ahead that welcome is not a one Sunday-a-year event, but an every-Sunday happening at Christ the Lord… a community opening to the world, welcoming every stranger, offering a cup of cold water to all who thirst.

AMDG

THE FAITH OF A CANAANITE DOG
A LECTIONARY SERMON FOR PENTECOST NINE 2011

But she came and knelt before him, saying, 'Lord, help me.' He answered, 'It is not fair to take the children's food and throw it to the dogs.'[107]

What a strange story we have today…Jesus in some strange place… outside Israel…acting very strangely. Is this the Jesus we know? The same compassionate Jesus we hear about every Sunday? Who is **this** Jesus who meets a woman on her knees, pleading for her child, and calls her a **dog**? Why? What's going on here?

Can't you sense the arrogance in Jesus' voice? The insult in his choice of words? A dog?! A woman on her knees…a dog?!

And where is this Tyre and Sidon? What is Jesus doing there? The questions just roll off every line of this story. They force us to look in new ways at Jesus at and the nature and power of faith.

Unfortunately, answers don't come anywhere near as easily. But, there **are** answers…or, at least, some suggestions of answers.

Let's begin by locating this place geographically. Tyre and Sidon are in the district of Phoenicia, on the coast of the Roman province of Syria… just north of the Roman province of Palestine…and, therefore, just outside the political reach of Herod and the religious authorities of the Pharisees, the Sanhedrin. On the maps of today they are in southern Lebanon. Then and now, the inhabitants were not, are not Jews. Today they are Arabs – Lebanese Muslims and Christians and Druze. In Mark's telling of this story, the woman is more accurately described as a Syro-phoenician, a Gentile. Then and now, however, these Syro-phoenicians - or Lebanese - lived and live close enough to Israel to understand the ways of Israelites and, now, Israelis, including the nature of Judaism…something the woman of this story demonstrated to Jesus by calling him "Lord, Son of David;" that is "Messiah." And, today, the inhabitants of this area are treated with the same arrogance by their neighbors to the south as they were in Jesus' time. In recent decades, they have twice been invaded and occupied by those neighbors and the cities of Tyre and Sidon more than twice reduced to rubble. You might say they continue to be treated like dogs.

So what brought Jesus to such a place? Surely not to preach and convert the local Gentiles. Didn't Jesus say: "I was sent only to the lost sheep of the house of Israel?"[108] Didn't he tell his disciples, as he sent them out, to keep their distance from Gentiles? Maybe he just wanted to get away from the crowds, the daily grind of preaching, teaching, healing. Maybe he just wanted some peace and quiet. Remember that story of the loaves and fishes two weeks ago? Remember what Susan said about how a grieving Jesus sought a quiet place to pray, to regain his strength for the road ahead? Remember last Sunday…Jesus seeking peace and quiet on a mountain after an exhausting day with that crowd? The suggestion by one commentator that today Jesus is just hopping across the border to seek some R&R might not be all that far-fetched.

Perhaps. More likely, however, he was "on the lam," hiding out from the authorities on his tail. Hadn't he – in last week's Gospel – just rebuked the Pharisees for their hypocrisy in valuing tradition more than the spiritual content of the word of God. Didn't the disciples – in the first verses of today's Gospel…the ones we didn't hear – warn Jesus, saying "Do you know that the Pharisees took offense when they heard what you said?"[109] Can't you hear them adding "We'd better get out of town."

And so we find Jesus and the disciples in the region of Tyre and Sidon…out of reach of Israel's religious police…probably exhausted… perhaps still a bit edgy from a close call. There they encounter this desperate mother, who, the disciples report "keeps shouting after us." "Get rid of her, Jesus, she's making a pest of herself." You want peace and quiet…and we get this…this…Canaanite.

And here we have the first putdown of this Syro-Phoenician woman, the first insult…a racial slur. Matthew's use here of the term "Canaanite" is telling. The Canaanites, the people who occupied Palestine when the Israelites first arrived, fresh from their own persecution in Egypt, were, in Jesus' time, considered less than human…ancient savage enemies whom, God ordained, deserved to be crushed and persecuted. Sound familiar? To call someone a Canaanite was like a cowboy in a B-movie hurling epithets at those ignorant, evil redskins who stood in the way of our Manifest Destiny. And, remember how we all cheered as those "savages" were gunned down in their faceless, nameless thousands? Weren't they **ours** to crush and persecute?

But it gets worse. Jesus' response to the woman's "Lord, help me," is "It is not fair to take the children's food" – the Israelites' food - "and throw it to the dogs" – the Canaanite dogs. Speaking of B-movies, remember those Gestapo thugs barking out their "*Schweinhund!*" – Pig Dog! - at some pleading Jew or half-conscious POW? Words hurt…and can sometimes kill… as when a seventh grader, repeatedly called a fag, a queer, or something worse, is found hanging in his room.

But this is Jesus. Surely *he* would not intentionally hurt anybody this way. Hold on to that thought, that word "*intentionally*," for just a moment. Now some commentators tell us that he would, of course, not hurt anybody, not intentionally. They point out that the Greek word he used for "dog," was more like "doggy" or "puppy," as in a house pet. You know, "Here Cocoa. Nice Cocoa."[110] My three years of Greek is now fifty-three years old and a bit rusty. So I won't even try disputing that contention. But it doesn't really matter, for mockery can sting just as surely as the outright slur. I can remember a time in this country when a white teenager could call a gray-haired black man "Boy" and expect a "Yessuh" in return. I have some idea what that seventh grader might feel being called "Sweetie Pie." And we all know from this book – our Bible - what followed after those wise-guy centurions placed a crown of thorns on a man's head, a purple robe on his bleeding shoulders, and bowed before "The King of The Jews," smirking, as the words curled off their lips. Yes, mockery, too, can kill.

But what probably hurt most in this story were not the condescending *words* of Jesus, but rather his initial silence – the very absence of words, her prayer unanswered. "He did not answer her at all," we are told. Haven't we all been there? Haven't we all prayed for some miracle, great or small… and hearing nothing in return, felt tuned out by God…abandoned by God? In that moment, haven't we felt crushed, unworthy, and – let's face it – resentful.

Maybe this Canaanite dog of a woman felt all those emotions. But she was different. Her love for her daughter was too great. Her faith – that she could change the heart of Jesus - was too great. And, so, too, were her persistence and resourcefulness. She was not about to roll over and crawl under anyone's table. She was not about to be anyone's obedient pet. She knew she was right and she knew she could break open the heart of God… the heart of God trapped in the very human body of a young Israelite…a body and mind burdened by the cultural baggage of millennia, by insularity, by disdain for Gentiles and, most especially, Canaanites…baggage that Jesus had to discard along the way on his journey to a full realization of his divinity.

A few moments ago, I asked you to hang on to that word "intentionally." Surely, Jesus *Christ* – the transfigured, risen Son of God – would not intentionally hurt anyone…despite the wishes of "men of God" like Pat Robertson, Jerry Falwell, or Fred Phelps. But I ask you to consider…whether a still young, very human carpenter from Nazareth - someone who had been carefully taught by his society to keep his distance from Gentiles and to despise Canaanites - might here slip and sting by his words? I ask you also to consider the faith of this Gentile Canaanite woman who saw far more in this miracle-working carpenter than perhaps he saw in himself. Consider also her persistence. She would not give up. She would show him what *she* saw…what *he* had to see. Consider finally her resourcefulness…how she went about that.

Consider how she gently turned the tables on Jesus. What an impressive example of verbal jiu jitsu, that comeback of hers - "even dogs eat the crumbs that fall from their masters' table." Even Jesus was impressed. And, reading between the lines, he might even have been amused. You know, "You got me. You win." Can't you see him smiling, as he answered "Woman, great is your faith! Let it be done for you as you wish."

"And her daughter was healed instantly." But that's not the only miracle that occurred that day. For, in that moment, she changed the heart of Jesus, she touched the heart of God. She expanded Jesus' vision, his horizon. She gave him perhaps new insight into his understanding of his divinity. And she expanded the size of his tent. No longer would his flock consist only of the "lost sheep of the house of Israel." Henceforth, it would include Gentiles. It would include us.

Without this Canaanite dog of a woman there would be no Paul, no mission to the Gentiles. You and I would probably not be Christians. For Christianity – in the form of a "new and improved" Judaism…a for-Jews-only "Christianity" – might not have spread beyond the borders of a tiny Roman province called Palestine. Born far outside those borders, oceans away, we might be pagans or adherents to some other religion that made it across the oceans that surround us. But we're not, because, in the end, the very end of Matthew's Gospel, Jesus, the now risen Christ, commanded his disciples to "Go therefore and make disciples of all nations…." The religion of Jesus was no longer the exclusivist stuff of Israel he took into Tyre and Sidon. It had become his wildly inclusive gift to all nations…to all people.

This Canaanite woman, whose name we'll never know, made a difference, a huge difference in the life of Jesus…and in **our** lives. She is someone worth emulating. Listen to today's writer in *Forward Day by Day*:

> The people who make a difference are often those who
> refuse to give in to authority when authority is unfair.
> They are persistent and creative and avoid getting trapped

into the expectation of "she's only a woman," "he's only
a foreigner, "she hasn't been properly educated," or
whatever else is said to demean people. Without such
persons the world would be worse off.

How I wish we knew her name, so we might properly sing her praise. Not knowing it, we're left to fall back on Ecclesiasticus…his "Hymn in honor of our ancestors." Somehow, I don't think he'll mind if I change the gender of those ancestors.

> Let us now sing the praises of famous women,
> our ancestors in their generations.
> Some of them have left behind a name,
> so that others declare their praise.
> But of others there is no memory;
> they have perished as though they had never existed;
> they have become as though they had never been born,
> they and their children after them.
> But these also were godly women,
> whose righteous deeds have not been forgotten…[111]

And so it is with Canaanite woman. Her "righteous deeds have [indeed] not been forgotten." For, across the millennia, the words of someone else have not been forgotten: "Woman, great is your faith!"

AMDG

136

TO FORGIVE AND...FORGET?
A SERMON FOR SEPTEMBER 11 TEN YEARS ON 2011

Forgive us our trespasses, as we
forgive those who trespass against us[112]

Good morning. Remembering the date, many of you are probably thinking "What's so good about it?" Remembering the date, aren't I supposed to ask "Where were you this morning ten years ago?" But, didn't we do that last year? Didn't I tell you where I was? Where my niece was in lower Manhattan? Didn't you think about where you were...and perhaps try to forget? Another year's gone by, a decade now. Have you been able to forget? To forgive? Do you want to? To forgive? To forget?

Today's Gospel is incredibly simple, but, oh, so hard. How simple? We are called to forgive...not once, not twice, not seven times, but, Jesus tells us, seventy-seven times...infinitely...always...*every* time. And how are we to forgive? We are to forgive as we would wish to be forgiven, as we *need* to be forgiven, as we pray to be forgiven: "Forgive us our trespasses, as we forgive those who trespass against us."

That passage of the Lord's Prayer, our prayer to our Father, has various wordings. In one, our "trespasses" become "debts" and, no matter the version, refer to sins. And, in today's Gospel, Jesus uses the debt analogy – an analogy those of us in this money-obsessed twenty-first century might especially understand. He turns those words from his prayer to his father into a parable...as if to say "Do you get it *now*?" It is a parable that can be understood in the nine little words from that prayer: "Forgive us our debts, as we forgive our debtors."

Simple right?

Simple? Have you ever had to forgive someone who raped your daughter…like Jaycee Dugard's parents? Someone who killed your brother…or mom or dad… some drunken driver on I-80, some faceless fighter in Afghanistan or Kurdistan? Then, there are those anger-crazed fanatics who drove three planes into three buildings and another into the ground…and killed three thousand of our sons and daughters, sisters and brothers, husbands and wives. Have you forgiven them? Can you? And what if the three thousand had been six million? What if you were a Jew? What if one of the six million had been your mom or dad? What if you had been in one of those death camps and survived? Could you forgive the German…the "Christian"…who pulled the trigger…or mindlessly opened the gas spigot?

For me, these are not academic questions that I studied in some seminary. They are questions that I've lived. For three years, I lived in Krakow, Poland…an hour from Auschwitz. I've walked that awful railroad track. I've peered into the ovens…and swear I could smell the stench of death. And, in Krakow 's old ghetto, I met the few survivors – a thousand of once a hundred thousand - and talked with them of those who hadn't survived. And later, I lived in Munich, the place Hitler called the *Hauptstadt der Bewegung*, the capital of the Nazi movement…a stone's throw from Dachau. There, I met many good Germans who resisted Hitler, some who may have survived with a wounded conscience, and, perhaps, more than one of the killers, survivors of another sort…the *Murderers among Us* that the famed Nazi hunter Simon Wiesenthal wrote about.[113]

But today I'd like to talk about another book by Wiesenthal – *The Sunflower*.[114] The first half of the book is a powerful parable on the "possibilities and limits of forgiveness." It relates a tale about Wiesenthal's time as a prisoner orderly in an SS hospital in Lvov in western Ukraine. There - alone in a hospital room - he encounters, Karl, a blinded, horribly burned German. The dying SS man, a lapsed Roman Catholic, summons Wiesenthal to his side and insists that he hear his confession…a graphic recitation of the hundreds of Jews he has killed. He begs for Wiesenthal's hand, his forgiveness. It is the German's final hope for atonement. Wiesenthal leaves the room in silence, withholding that forgiveness – a non-act that haunts Wiesenthal the rest of his life. And *we* are left to struggle with the question posed on the cover of the book: "What would you do?"

Again, it all seems *sooo* simple. Some of us, fingering perhaps the "WWJD" on some rubber bracelet, would confidently pose another question: "What would Jesus do?" Of course, he'd forgive the dying murderer. Didn't he forgive his own killers? Of course, he'd forgive the terrorist, shouting his "Allah u Ahkba," as he flew his plane into the 82nd floor. Wouldn't he say again: "Father, forgive them; for they do not know what they are doing?" Of course, he would.

But that's the wrong question. The proper question, the one we're asked today is: What would Jesus have *us* do…in our imperfections, with our limitations, with our lust for vengeance? That's a much harder question. And the answer is nowhere near as certain.

In *The Sunflower*, the question on the cover of the book becomes the stuff of a symposium that is the second half of the book. It becomes the question that more than forty leaders of the faith and moral community – Christians, Jews, Muslims, Buddhists, agnostics, and non-believers – are called to grapple with – "What would you do?"

It is a question *I've* grappled with over a long lifetime, as I've contemplated the words of Jesus, the reflections in *The Sunflower*, and real life situations that have challenged me to give and to seek forgiveness. It is a question we all grapple with again this morning as we consider – perhaps for the first time in a long time - the events of September 11, our reactions to them, and what Jesus would have us do in their wake. As we do, let me share some random thoughts from my own struggle with this question of giving and seeking forgiveness.

First, there is the matter of perspective. Jesus draws our attention to it in today's parable in terms of dollars and cents…or talents and denarii. It's no accident that here the one who owes ten thousand talents – an impossible sum to repay, since one talent was tantamount to fifteen years' wages – is unwilling to forgive the debt of a fellow slave who owed but a hundred denarii or three months' wages. Were he to rephrase this as a parable, not on debts, but on deaths - deaths visited on one another from the sky - might not Jesus ask us, as we pray in our sorrow for the 3,000 dead of September 11, also to mourn - if just silently - the 6,000 killed in Baghdad's "shock and awe," the 25,000 in Dresden, the 50,000 in the fire raids on Hamburg, the 90,000 in the fire raids on Tokyo, and the 200,000 in Hiroshima and Nagasaki. If we have sought and received forgiveness for 300,000 such deaths from a merciful God, can we not find it in our hearts to forgive those who killed 3,000 of our kinfolk? Do we really mean it, when we pray "Forgive us our debts, as we forgive our debtors," "Forgive us our trespasses, as we forgive who trespass against us?"

This is not to put human lives in the same category as debts measured in talents and denarii, dollars and cents, or any numbers…nor to place those lives on some perverse scales that value one of ours as a hundred of theirs. No, each life is infinitely valuable…to God and to us. Just as some among us may mourn the death of an individual friend or family member who died on September 11, so, too, there are Afghanis and Iraqis who mourn someone they love who died since then. There was a rabbi who said "If you take one life, you kill all mankind."[115] And to do that is profoundly evil.

And, make no mistake about it, what happened on 9/11 was profoundly evil. If, in working for the Kingdom of God, we seek to usher in God's heaven on earth, those who steered those planes into the World Trade Center opened the gates of hell; they loosed hell on earth. What is hell? Consider those people on the 102nd floor – the waiters at Windows on the World, the brokers at Cantor Fitzgerald, the janitors – unable to breathe the black smoke, the flames licking at their backs, holding hands in a last act of human solidarity…and leaping – willfully, courageously – to their deaths, hoping perhaps to wake up in heaven. I have no doubt, however, that, for one excruciating moment, they experienced all the pain of hell for all the eternity that is in a moment.

But, even if we're inclined to forgive such horror, is it within our power to do so? Some in *The Sunflower* discussion think not. Wiesenthal himself says he could not forgive the SS-man, because his were not crimes committed against Wiesenthal personally, but against others. Eva Fleischner, another Jew, agrees, pointing out that the Lord's Prayer says "Forgive us our trespasses, as we forgive those who trespass against ***us***," not, she adds, "those who trespass against others."[116] And, according to the great Rabbi Abraham Heschel, no one can forgive crimes committed against other people ***by*** other people. "It is," he says, "therefore preposterous to assume that anybody alive can extend forgiveness for the suffering of any one of the six million people who perished."[117] Or, one might add, the three thousand who died on September 11th.

Heschel goes one step further, citing Jewish tradition that "even God himself can only forgive sins against himself not against man"[118]… to which Matthew Fox, an Episcopal priest, adds that "no one had anointed Simon to forgive in God's name."[119] But Father Theodore Hesburgh, then president emeritus of Notre Dame, disagrees:

> My whole instinct is to forgive. Perhaps that is because I am a Catholic priest. In a sense, I am in the forgiving business…Of course, the sin here is monumental. It is still finite and God's mercy is infinite. If asked to forgive, by anyone for anything, I would forgive because God would forgive.[120]

So would I. I'm a Christian. And, we, too, are in the forgiving business.

I would also question the line Fleischner so crisply, so simply draws between "us" and "others" in dissecting the Lord's Prayer. For neither does it say "Forgive ***me my*** trespasses, as ***I*** forgive those who trespass against ***me***." Who, I would ask, do we understand as "***us***," as "***we***," in the context of the Holocaust, September 11, the Lord's Prayer? Was the Holocaust a crime only against those killed…or against ***all*** Jews, dead and alive? Did the hijackers of September 11 seek only to kill three thousand or to instill a crippling fear in the hearts of **all** Americans? And when crimes of such magnitude are committed against anyone anywhere, are they not crimes against us all in our shared humanity. I've said it again and again. Let me say it once more: We find our salvation, not in solitude, but in community.

But, **why** forgive? What's in it for us…to make easier our journey together through this life, toward salvation? In forgiving, Jesus tells us, we heap coals upon the heads of our enemies. But, think about it, isn't that a form of vengeance, of passive aggression? Is that sufficient motive forgiving? But, think also of the obverse – **withholding** our forgiveness. When we do not forgive, do we not heap coals upon our own heads? Do we not allow our pain, our hurt, our sense of victimhood, to fester, to grow, and eventually explode in some self-defeating act of violence? In doing so, do we not allow our fears and anger to drive out our hopes and dreams? Do we not allow our dreams to become our worst nightmares? Listen to Langston Hughes:

What happens to a dream deferred?

> Does it dry up
> like a raisin in the sun?
> Or fester like a sore--
> And then run?
> Does it stink like rotten meat?
> Or crust and sugar over--
> like a syrupy sweet?
> Maybe it just sags
> like a heavy load.
> Or does it explode?[121]

Isn't that what happened **after** 9/11? Didn't we allow our fear and anger to drive out our hopes and dreams, our better spirits…to explode in the paroxysm of violence that has marked the last decade? Didn't we choose vengeance over forgiveness? Didn't we close our eyes to the words of Paul from just two weeks ago – "Do not repay anyone evil for evil….never avenge yourselves, but leave room for the wrath of God; for it is written,

'Vengeance is mine'....Do not be overcome by evil, but overcome evil with good?"[122]

And, in choosing vengeance, didn't we allow a dozen dead terrorists to heap coals on our heads – two wars, two and three times longer than World War II; two wars that have resulted in more dead young Americans than were killed on September 11; many tens of thousands of families dealing with the life-altering wounds of battle; hundreds of thousands of dead Iraqis and Afghanis and millions more who hate us for killing *their* brothers and sisters; six trillion dollars mindlessly squandered on all the killing; an economy in shambles; our ostracism of the vulnerable Other; the endemic fear that paralyzes. Are *these* not *also* trespasses for which *we* should seek the forgiveness of millions of faceless strangers? Are they not debts for which we need seek forgiveness from our children and our generations as yet unborn? Are they not sins for which we must seek forgiveness from God?

If we are to find such forgiveness, if we are to live together - perpetrators and victims - in a peaceful present, we must break free of the cycle of violence that holds us in its thrall. And, that requires facing the sometimes hard truths that must precede reconciliation. Such remembrance, thoughtfully embraced, can yield remarkable reconciliation, as it has in South Africa, Chile, and post-communist Europe. When, however, the truth of past injustice is swept under the rug – as in the former Yugoslavia, in Israel/Palestine, or pre-1960s America – it produces the sorts of explosions Langston Hughes had so very much in mind.

No, forgiveness does not mean forgetting. We are called, rather, to remember…to never forget the sting of the pain and the injustice visited upon us… so that we do not visit it upon others. Jews, in particular, have been called to remember the Exodus we have been recalling these many weeks and again this morning…to remember that they – that we - were once slaves in Egypt, to remember to be hospitable to the fellow sojourners in our midst. And, in remembering the horrors of the Holocaust, they and we are all called to live into the meaning of those two words – Never again!

Never again…not for us…or ***anyone***.

It is a vow that is being sorely tested in the Holy Land this very week as Israelis and Palestinians, Christians, Jews, and Muslims confront yet another round in the seemingly unending tit-for-tat, eye-for-eye, tooth-for-tooth cycle of violence. It is a situation that cries to heaven for mutual forgiveness, for justice, reconciliation, and peace.

In a few minutes, we will add our voices to that cry, that rising prayer, as we place this tiny dove of peace on our altar and light its flame of olive oil from the hills of Ephraim that offered Jesus refuge in another time of strife.

As we do so, on this somber anniversary, let us seize this moment as the "opportunity for reflection" that Katharine, our Presiding Bishop has called us to. "Have we become," she asks, "more effective reconcilers as a result? Are we more committed to peace-making?" "The greatest memorial to those who died ten years ago," she says, "will be a world more inclined toward peace." "What, she asks, "are you doing to build a living memorial like that?"[123]

To Katharine's question, to those of Simon Wiesenthal, of Langston Hughes, of that silent voice in your heart this morning, let me add, let me close, with just one more…from a drunken driver beaten senseless beside a Los Angeles Freeway. In the wake of the acquittal of his attackers, in the midst of the riots that had already taken thirty-five lives, a bewildered, tearful Rodney King asked: "People, I just want to say, you know, can we all get along? Can we get along? Can we stop making it, making it horrible for the older people and the kids?...It's just not right. It's not right. It's not…"[124]

AMDG

CHRIST, OUR SHEPHERD KING
A LECTIONARY SERMON FOR PENTECOST
TWENTY-THREE 2011

Know that the LORD is God.
It is he that made us, and we are his;
we are his people, and the sheep of his pasture.[125]

Happy Birthday to us,
Happy Birthday to us,
Happy Birthday, Christ the Lord,
Happy Birthday to us.

Yes, today is our birthday, our feast day. But no mere patron saint for us. Our patron is God himself, herself in the body of Jesus, Christ, our Shepherd King.

We are all of forty-three, having been founded in 1968. It was, as some of us are old enough to remember, a year that was the best of times and the worst of times. There were those who fought for human dignity and were gunned down in their youth. There was violence in foreign jungles and on our city streets...and there were those who marched for peace. There was the ever-present threat of nuclear annihilation...and our first view of our blue island home and the voice of an astronaut reading on Christmas Eve from the Book of Genesis. There was the pain of so much hope snuffed out in Paris, Berlin, Prague, and Chicago. And the whole world was watching.

The whole world is watching again...for we are again on that cusp between hope and despair. We have experienced forty-three years of endless war – overlapping, futile, and, for the most part, unworthy wars...wars that have left us mired in Afghanistan and facing perceived enemies on every continent. We are suffering the consequence of decades of rampant greed and reckless risk-taking that have produced a Great Recession in an America we hardly recognize any more.

And the powers-that-be of this world again seek to block the change we need - banks that gambled with our savings and took our homes, corporations that export our jobs, politicians who spout focus-group tested one-liners and fiddle while a nation burns, corporate media that would distract us from the fire with daily offerings of circus-like "infotainment." The results are an income inequality not seen since 1928, in which 40 percent of the nation's wealth is held by one percent of our people; real unemployment near 16 percent; an increasingly less progressive tax system unworthy of a civilized society; rampant cuts in programs for the suffering among us; a people on its knees.

As we struggle to stand, we hear this morning, in Ezekiel, the voice of hope, the voice of God, the voice of our Shepherd King. "I will seek out my sheep," God promises us. "I will rescue them from all the places to which they have been scattered on a day of clouds and thick darkness…. I will seek the lost, and I will bring back the strayed, and I will bind up the injured, and I will strengthen the weak, but the fat and the strong I will destroy. I will feed them with justice."[126]

And of those who have led us to this place of clouds and darkness – the haughty, greedy, self-centered, self-satisfied powers-that-be on Wall Street and in Washington – our Shepherd King asks in anger in the central, but strangely omitted heart of today's reading: "Is it not enough for you to feed on the good pasture, but must you also tread down with your feet the rest of your pasture? When you drink of clear water, must you foul the rest with your feet? And must my sheep eat what you have trodden with your feet, and drink what you have fouled with your feet?"[127] "No!" God tells us. He will judge between the fat sheep – the fat cats - who have "pushed with flank and shoulder, and butted at all the weak animals" and the lean sheep, the rest of us…the 99%. "I will save my flock," he assures us, "and they shall no longer be ravaged."

Let me say this as clearly and forcefully as I can, Christ, our Shepherd King has a strong preference for the lean sheep, for the least of his flock. Indeed, as Jesus tells us today in Matthew, he is the leanest among us, the least of us. He has his hand out to us.

To be sure, Jesus does not begrudge anyone the fair fruits of honest labor. But he has little patience with those who would use the advantage thus gained to hoard more than their fair share or to lord it over those in need, to further disadvantage them. To all of us – rich or poor – Jesus posits just one measure of our righteousness:

> I was hungry and you gave me food, I was thirsty and
> you gave me something to drink, I was a stranger and
> you welcomed me, was naked and you gave me
> clothing, I was sick and you took care of me, I was in
> prison and you visited me." Then the righteous will
> answer him, "Lord, when was it that we saw you hungry
> and gave you food, or thirsty and gave you something to
> drink? And when was it that we saw you a stranger and
> welcomed you, or naked and gave you clothing? And
> when was it that we saw you sick or in prison and visited
> you?" And the king will answer them, "Truly I tell you,
> just as you did it to one of the least of these who are
> members of my family, you did it to me."[128]

And, as Obery Hendricks, a distinguished Professor of Biblical Interpretation, tells us:

> By the measure Jesus gives us here, it is not religious
> practice, or memorization of scriptures, or even faithful
> attendance at church or temple by which our lives will
> be judged. It is simply whether we have tried to relieve
> the plight of the hungry and dispossessed and those
> stripped of their freedom; whether we have tried to change
> this war-torn world to a world free from oppression and
> exploitation, so that all of God's children might have life,

and that more abundantly. [129]

To those of us who try – to feed the hungry, give drink to the thirsty, welcome the stranger, clothe the naked, visit those sick or in prison - Christ our King promises that we will "inherit the kingdom prepared for you from the foundation of the world."[130] And, what, we ask, is the nature of that kingdom?

For the late, great Peter Gomes, who wrote and preached from the perspective of the Social Gospel advanced toward the end of the first Gilded Age in America, a time of robber barons and sweatshops a century and more ago, the answer is clear. For the preachers of the time, he tells us, "the 'kingdom of God' was not simply some faraway and/or theoretical eschatological enterprise located either in heaven or at the end of the age; it was something to be brought into being in this world by the application of Christian principles to the least in society. The Gospel was social in that it was too important to be left alone in the church…"[131]

And one has the sense, at the end of this current Gilded Age, this time of rampant greed and rampant poverty, that *that* is precisely the task of the church - to bust through our confining walls and take that Gospel – the Good News – out that door to wherever God's children are huddled in their pain, their fear, their yearning. One has the sense, however, that, as the Occupy movement unfolds and grows, the church has been slow to catch on, to heed the call of our humble Shepherd King. It's as if we're only very slowly awakening from a long sleep.

But we *are* stirring. On Thursday Maria Isabel Santiviago, vicar of St. Ann's Church for the Deaf in New York, joined the marchers on the Brooklyn Bridge during the Global Day of Action to mark the movement's two-month anniversary. Before Occupy, she told Episcopal News Service, "we were, like zombies … this is a wake up."[132]

That same day, five Episcopal churches in Manhattan opened their doors to the "dislocated occupiers," who had been brutally rousted from Zucotti Park just the day before, and seminarians from General Theological Seminary, wearing cassocks and armed with anointing oil, joined peaceful protesters at a subway station.

In Portland, our own Josh Griffin, now at St. David of Wales, has married his climate justice sensibilities to Occupy's targeting of big banks. "This," he told Episcopal News Service during one such action Thursday, "is not a protest movement, it is public liturgy of the finest sort. This movement is powerful because it is showing us a way forward."[133]

And Thursday night, as we waited in the drizzle for a rumored police crackdown, these were messages that resonated on Justin Herman Plaza among the small circle of speakers seeking courage in community – union members, Veterans for Peace, students crushed by college debt, the newly homeless, those long homeless and hungry, some talented musicians, a young lawyer, a fire department paramedic, Diamond Dave and Dr. B... and not nearly enough clergy.

It came my turn to speak. My words were short and simple: "This is something the church – my church – should have been doing a long time ago. Thank you for leading us. Thank you for showing us what we should be doing. Stay strong. We're with you!" And the crowd said: "Amen!"

And I will return tonight, when members of the Council of Elders, leaders of the 20th Century movements for civil rights and social justice will pass the torch to the 21st Century leaders of Occupy in New York, Los Angeles, Oakland, and San Francisco. In doing so, they seek to affirm "the continuation and...expansion of the movement toward the Beloved Community - a more compassionate, just and democratic society." Having participated in those movements of the sixties and drawing new energy from today's, I feel a need to be a bridge of sorts - like much of our infrastructure, creaking a bit, but still usable – between the generations and between the church and a hurting world. I hope some of you will join me - 5:30, Justin Herman Plaza, Embarcadero BART. This creaking bridge needs some shoring up.

And I feel a special need to join the crowd on Justin Herman Plaza to hear the strong voice of a hero of mine – the eighty-something veteran of the civil rights movement, Vincent Harding. Who is Vincent Harding? He was a close associate of Martin's and wrote several of his speeches. One was Martin's 1967 Riverside speech opposing the Vietnam War. It contains the memorable line: "There is a time when silence is betrayal."

There is, indeed, and it has come again.

Josh Griffin, that twenty-something priest in Portland has said it well: "Occupy is changing the public discourse and refocusing our attentions where they should be." "I think," he said, "our church needs to have a very serious conversation; it's completely embedded and dependent on the exploitative economy, based on the extraction and consumption of resources. We need to figure out how to free ourselves from those dependencies."[134]

Church is not a building. It is not just a time on Sunday morning. It is people...people in community...the sort of community that came together in 1968 in Pinole...the sort of community that is learning anew how to be Christ's hands and feet and heart in the world...the sort of community that is breaking down walls, plowing new fields, sowing new seed.

In a few minutes I will add my thanksgiving leaf to our tree. It reads: "For the walls we're breaking down."

Happy Birthday! Keep swinging that hammer.

AMDG

SPEAK, FOR YOUR SERVANT IS LISTENING
A SERMON ON MARTIN'S BIRTHDAY 2012

Here I am … Speak, Lord, for your servant is listening.[135]

I'm always grateful for the opportunity to preach on Martin's birthday. I recall I did last year, too…and in other years in other churches. I'm especially glad for the opportunity to do so ***this*** year.

We're so different in so many ways, Martin and I. He was a man, I'm a woman. He was black, I'm white. He was a prophet who spoke from the nation's most prominent pulpits. I'm just a deacon who has only a small lectern in a small suburban church. He was killed for speaking the truth. I'm still grappling with it…still asking "What is truth?"

But I still cling to the central truth we share. We both listened. We both heard a voice that said "Follow me." And, one hot August day, we marched together.

I'm still marching…more slowly to be sure, sometimes wobbly, but still putting one foot ahead of the other. And that entails an obligation – an obligation we ***all*** have if we are to be found free of deceit …an obligation to seek the truth and speak it always…an obligation, as we vowed again last Sunday, to persevere in resisting evil; to proclaim not just by word but by example the Good News of God in Christ; to seek and serve Christ in all persons, loving our neighbors as ourselves; and an obligation to strive for justice and peace among all people, and respect the dignity of every human being.

So, how do we live into those vows? We cannot do so without risking our comfort, courting danger, causing trouble. As James Cone, the eminent theologian of Black Liberation, says, "If you're gonna worship somebody that was nailed to a tree, you must know that the life of a disciple of that person is not going to be easy." We cannot rest...nor think only of *moi*, when so many neighbors go unloved, when so many suffer countless daily indignities, when there is such an absence of justice and peace in the land... and such a surplus of evil.

And, in this winter of our discontent, the truth of that evil is manifest. We are trapped in the clutches of those who worship another god – the golden calf of greed – of the wealthy few who think not of "we," but only "me," and cause great pain to a wounded people in a wounded land.

And, adding to our discontent – at least to mine – the church, which should be leading the way out of this moral cul de sac, has been largely silent – even dismissive – as others seek to point the way.

I feel a need this morning to talk about the church, and how well – or even whether - we're listening, following, leading. We have to talk about how – this winter – the church is responding to – or isn't – to the pain in the land and how we relate – or don't – to the Occupy movement that has opened the conversation about that pain.

For my part, I feel that it's urgent for the church get off the sidelines and embrace the Occupy movement. For it seeks the same over-arching goal we say we do - a society that is fair and just and loving...a Beloved Community of Shalom. Our legitimacy is on the line. Do we truly believe Jesus' words and ours? Are we prepared to speak and act - dangerously - on our beliefs?

Young people, in particular, are waiting for our answers and, I assure you, anxious to embrace us. Having spent three months now among them in Justin Herman Plaza, at 101 Market, on a trolley track in the middle of Market Street, in visioning group meetings, at general assemblies, in myriad actions, and breaking bread together on Black Friday and Christmas Day, I have found them calling us to do what we as a church should have been doing a long time ago. Are we listening?

Charity is good and necessary, but never sufficient. We have to move beyond the reactive salving of the wounds inflicted on the weakest in a very sick society. We have to move beyond the consequences and address the causes of our dis-ease. We have to move from staunching the bleeding to taking the sword out of the hand of those doing the cutting. In our hearts of hearts, we know who are doing the cutting and how it's done. And we know it's not fair. That is the message of Occupy...and its challenge - "Do something! Do something about it!"

By my lights, we failed miserably in not doing so with open arms and open hearts in New York. We continue to do so – to do next to nothing - here and around the nation. And, this being an episcopal church, the bishops bear a large share of the blame.

Expressing "alarm" at Occupy's attempts to gain access to Trinity's Duarte Square and using language reminiscent of what Dr. King heard in Birmingham, New York's Bishop Sisk said that "the movement should not be used to justify breaking the law." He further called for "peaceful articulation, in word and deed, of the issues of justice and fairness that have brought the Occupy movement into the national conversation."[136] Unfortunately, in saying that, the bishop confused the cart with the horse, for it has, of course, been Occupy that has brought justice and fairness into the national conversation.

And, in an accompanying statement the week before Christmas, the Presiding Bishop chided Occupy for "attempting to trespass" on Trinity property, adding that "seekers after justice have more often achieved success through non-violent action, rather than acts of force or arms."[137] That unfortunately ignores Occupy's commitment and general adherence to non-violence in the face of the acts of force and arms employed by the authorities in New York, Oakland, UC Davis, San Francisco and wherever Occupy has sought peacefully to assemble. In closing, she urged Occupy "to stand down and seek justice in ways that do not further alienate potential allies." In other words, be nice. Forgive me, I cannot recall Jesus ever telling us to be nice with or to refrain from alienating the powers-that-be in seeking of justice.

Meanwhile, here in the Bay Area, our own Bishop Marc has refrained from public statements on the unfolding events in Oakland, Berkeley, and Justin Herman Plaza. He has instead ruminated on his blog about the slowly evolving nature of a transformative social movement such as this. Expressing a preference for "deliberation," he sees, he says, no need "to hurry and make my point or act right away or I will have missed all the action" "My deliberation" he has blogged, "is an act of faith that Martin Luther King, Jr. was right when he said that the arc of history bends towards justice. Or, put another way, the mills of the Lord grind slow but exceeding fine."[138]

Perhaps, but Martin also wrote from that Birmingham City Jail - to fellow clergy who advised him to take his time, to avoid breaking laws, and to act with propriety - "For years now I have heard the word 'Wait!' It rings in the ear of every Negro with piercing familiarity. This 'Wait' has almost always meant 'Never.' We must come to see, with one of our distinguished jurists, that 'justice too long delayed is justice denied.'"[139]

And, about the church, Martin wrote:

> The contemporary church so often is a weak, ineffectual
> voice with an uncertain sound. So often it is an arch
> defender of the status quo. Far from being disturbed by
> the presence of the church, the power structure of the
> average community is consoled by the church's silent
> and often even vocal sanction of things as they are.

> But the judgment of God is upon the church as never
> before. If today's church does not recapture the sacrificial
> spirit of the early church, it will lose its authenticity,
> forfeit the loyalty of millions, and be dismissed as an
> irrelevant social club with no meaning for the twentieth
> century. Every day I meet young people whose
> disappointment with the church has turned into outright
> disgust.

Perhaps I have once again been too optimistic. Is
organized religion too inextricably bound to the status
quo to save our nation and the world? Perhaps I must turn
my faith to the inner spiritual church, the church within
the church, as the true ekklesia and the hope of the world.
But again I am thankful to God that some noble souls
from the ranks of organized religion have broken loose
from the paralyzing chains of conformity and joined us as
active partners in the struggle for freedom.[140]

Our church remains an episcopal church, but it is one with more than just bishops or ordained ministers. We are *all* ministers, called to follow – called to lead - by our Baptism. Perhaps it is time – *for us* - to reach into that "inner spiritual church," to take our place among those "noble souls" who break the "paralyzing chains of conformity" and join - explicitly, physically - "in the struggle for freedom."

Might we not respond from the extravagant perspective of the Gospel of abundance rather than from the fearful, grudging stance of a church too closely, too long, associated with the powers-that-be, be they on Wall Street, Lafayette Square...or Nob Hill. Might we open our hearts to the yearnings of a new generation that sees its future slipping away? Might we welcome them into our buildings for physical respite and for nourishing conversation? Might we venture out of our buildings and join them in spiritual communion at 101 Market, at the Rincon Center, wherever Occupy comes together …and, together, become the change we seek.

There is a spiritual under-pinning to this movement that is palpable and that cries out for expression. We are at a critical moment. I lived through an earlier one in 1968 and sense again that what we do now will be determinative for a long time of the future of our country, our church, and our individual spiritual journeys. This is not one I can sit out. I hope you won't either.

There is a voice speaking. It has been speaking for two thousand years. Indeed, it has *always* been speaking. It is saying "Follow me!" Won't you listen? Won't you stand up? Won't you say "Here I am."

AMDG

OUR COMMON MINISTRY
A LECTIONARY SERMON FOR LAST SUNDAY
OF EPIPHANY 2012

He picked up the mantle of Elijah that had fallen from him,
and went back and stood on the bank of the Jordan.[141]

What an expectant moment. The start of a new ministry always is. It's a good place to pause, as we end the season of Epiphany and prepare for Lent that begins on Wednesday. And, as we do so, there's a lot to consider this morning – that chariot of fire, the torch passed to young Elisha, and Christ revealed at last in all his radiant glory as the Messiah. And, my little pocket calendar tells me this is also Reformation Sunday, that annual celebration of Martin Luther, and, in *our* church, World Mission Sunday. There's a lot to digest, but it's all about one thing – mission, ministry – Elisha's ministry, Christ's, Luther's…and ours. The main thing is the main thing is the main thing.

Let's begin with Martin Luther… his church, ours, and the Roman Catholic Church from whence *we* emerged as a church and from whence so many of us – myself included - came as individuals. Let's consider how our three churches inter-act…and to what end.

Last week Susan talked about her time in seminary and a term paper on Mark. Allow me this week to talk about my time at the School for Deacons and one of *my* favorite courses - church history.

And what a history it has been - often twisted; sometimes thunderous and bloody; on some occasions, unworthy; on others, soaring to inspiring heights; and, despite the conflicts and divisions and the small-mindedness of some, always moving forward, always on a mission.

The Sixteenth Century was a pivotal one in that history. In just five years, for example, we'll mark the 500th anniversary of Martin Luther taking hammer in hand and nailing his 95 Theses to the door of Wittenberg's *Schlosskirche*, a defiant act that sparked the Protestant Reformation.

Luther, a conscience-driven Augustinian monk, was particularly outraged by the church's sale of indulgences – chits which the church assured the buyer would shorten the time one had to spend in Purgatory enduring physical torment for already-forgiven sins. Adding insult to injury in Luther's mind, these indulgences, which had once been sold to finance the very-worldly Crusades, were, in his time, being sold to finance the very-worldly renovation of St. Peter's Basilica.

No such issues of conscience surrounded the break of our English or Anglican Church from Rome two decades later. Indeed, the precipitate affair – a not inappropriate word here – was the Pope's refusal to annul the marriage of Henry the Eighth to Catharine of Aragon, the first of his six wives…this, while he had already begun a dalliance with his would-be second wife, Anne Boleyn. I recall in this regard a poster of a very rotund Henry the Eighth that hung at the top of the office stairs in my last church, St. James in San Francisco. It bore the inscription "Would a church founded by this man be judgmental?"

To be sure, the issues of conscience that so enflamed Germany and the rest of the Continent soon found their way into England…into the space created by Henry's break with Rome…with equally bloody strife among the Puritans and other Protestants, Roman Catholics rallying under Mary Queen of Scots, and the new and immediately beleaguered Church of England. Enter Elizabeth and the solution that brought peace to England and that has held us together as Anglicans for nearly five-hundred years – the so-called *Via Media* or "middle way" that rests on that three-legged stool of Scripture – in the local language and accessible to all; Tradition – particularly in terms of apostolic succession and liturgy; and Reason – or freedom of conscience.

It is perhaps that last leg – freedom of conscience – that differentiates us most markedly from Roman Catholicism and the teaching authority of its Magisterium. For, according to the *Catechism of the Catholic Church*: "The task of interpreting the Word of God authentically has been entrusted **solely** to the Magisterium of the Church, that is, to the Pope and to the bishops in communion with him." The bishops have the power to tell you what you **must** believe…and sometimes they do…sometimes at the risk of excommunication.

This has been perhaps the chief cause of migration from the Roman to the Anglican Church. Indeed, it was a 1968 encyclical of Pope Paul VI – *Humane Vitae*, "On Human Life" – and a subsequent letter read from American pulpits that threatened those who practiced artificial birth control with eternal damnation that sent Mimi and me packing. And I must say I find it mind-blowing - forty-four years after that encyclical and forty-seven after Griswold v. Connecticut - that something so basic to privacy, the dignity and inviolability of one's body, and freedom of conscience is again the subject of instruction from **any** pulpit.

But, lest we become too smug or too self-righteous, keep in mind that migration from one church to another is a two-way street. As we know there are Episcopalians who are leaving to go to the Roman Catholic Church, to other churches, or, as with too many young people, to none. Those who have left our ranks for the Roman Catholic Church generally fall into two categories.

The first group, which includes some from the breakaway American Anglican Council and Convocation of Anglicans in North America, emphasizes its substantive differences with the Episcopal Church regarding the primacy and interpretation of Scripture, particularly with regard to sex and gender. These disaffected Episcopalians read Scripture more literally than we do and are apparently more comfortable in a church where gays and lesbians are closeted, where I am but a figment of my imagination, and where women need not apply for ordination. I wish them God-speed…and peace.

Then there are those who are more attracted by the tug of Tradition and more ancient forms of worship. High Church Episcopalians - Anglo-Catholics - for example, find special comfort in ornate liturgy. How ornate? Beyond bells and whistles, there are actually some Anglo-Catholic churches - in this diocese - that are so "high" that they regularly say Mass in Latin – a traditional liturgy that, until very recently, had gone out of favor even in the Roman Catholic Church.

Seeking to attract recruits from those in the Episcopal Church who, for whatever reason, might be more traditional, Pope Benedict has established an "Ordinariate," headed in this country by the former Episcopal bishop of the Rio Grande. This ordinairate welcomes married priests – men only of course – and allows parishes they head to continue Anglican liturgical flourishes and prayers. This has led the Archbishop of Canterbury to complain that Benedict is "poaching" for priests.

I'm here to tell you, however, as a member of our diocesan Commission on Ministry, that *we* have welcomed more than a few Roman Catholic priests into the Episcopal Church. And, as an individual, I also have to reiterate how grateful – how *eternally* grateful – I am that the Episcopal Church has provided a home for so many of us for whom the worship of God requires our whole heart, our whole soul, and *our whole mind*.

Before I found rest in this home, however, there were a few years – from 1968 to 1971 - when I belonged to neither the Roman Catholic nor the Episcopal Church. Work took me to Berlin and I found myself worshipping in a Lutheran church – the neighborhood *evangelische Kirche* of Berlin-Dahlem…Martin Niemöller's old church.

It was an important time for me…professionally, personally, spiritually. I learned a lot about the world and the power of people to endure oppression. And I learned a lot about church and what it should be. Daily, my work took me to East Berlin, to the other side of the Wall, to listen to young people and churchgoers tell their stories about personal and spiritual survival under an oppressively totalitarian communist regime.

And, in West Berlin, I absorbed the history of my little village church under another totalitarian regime and learned the story of its heroic pastor during Germany's *Nazizeit*. Martin Niemöller, was the leader of the "Confessing Church," the *Bekennede Kirche*, which resisted Hitler and Berlin's Reichsbishop Müller who threw in with the Nazis. Indeed, at a fateful National Synod, Müller demanded that every pastor sign an oath committing to the spiritual as well as political leadership of Adolf Hitler.

The response of the Confessing Church was swift and bold. At an assembly of over two thousand, the following declaration was read:

> This so-called national synod of Berlin and its decisions and deliberations are all invalid...The Reich church government despises the simple fundamentals of law and justice...It is devoid of that brotherly love made obligatory by the Holy Scriptures...He who consciously breaks laws which it is his personal duty to defend has foregone the...right to expect obedience. Obedience to this church government is disobedience to God.[142]

Someone who was in the hall that day described the response.

> Upon the reading of this bold declaration, those who were prepared to approve it were asked to stand. The congregation rose as one and sang Luther's great hymn, "A Mighty Fortress Is Our God." Their voices rang out strong and clear as they came to those words:
>
> > Let goods and kindred go,
> > This mortal life also,
> > The body they may kill,
> > God's truth abideth still,
> > His kingdom is forever.
>
> For them that was anything but mere rhetoric.[143]

I still get goose bumps when I sing that hymn. It brings back memories of that little church in Berlin-Dahlem and its one-time pastor who, at a difficult time, understood what ministry means.

It reminds me, too, how twelve years ago the Episcopal Church and the Evangelical Lutheran Church of America signed an agreement – "Called to Common Mission" - to share clergy, ministry and sacraments. It reminds me also of the continuing efforts of the Anglican Communion and the Roman Catholic Church to reach a similar agreement. And I have to believe – despite the setbacks and vicissitudes that have dogged those negotiations – that they too will bear fruit. For our common mission – our shared ministry – is far too important. The main thing is the main thing is the main thing. We are all Christians. And we are all called to ministry.

I believe it was Notre Dame's Knute Rockne who liked to say "When the going gets tough, the tough get going," Isn't that what we're being told this morning in Mark's Gospel and in our reading from Kings? Isn't that what Elijah and Jesus were saying…" There may be tough times ahead and I may not be there any longer to lead you physically, but you're up to it, you can do it"? There comes a time when the torch must be passed. And there are always new ministers to take it and carry it forward. Elisha picked up Elijah's cloak. So, too, did, Peter, James and John…carry forth the light they had seen and found a church. So, too, did Martin Luther…rekindle that light when it seemed but a smoldering wick. So, too, did Martin Niemöller and Dietrich Bonhoeffer who carried high the cross – even to death - when to do so was a crime. So, too did Martin Luther King, Jr. and Desmond Tutu who gave hope and dignity to God's suffering people.

And now it is our turn. As Paul tells us, "the god of this world has blinded the minds of the unbelievers, to keep them from seeing the light of the gospel of the glory of Christ, who is the image of God." The truth of that light is no longer a secret. Peter, James, and John saw it on a mountaintop and, through Mark, have told us. We are empowered. We no longer have any excuse. The torch that is that light is being held out to us. It's our turn. Take it. Take it out to our community, to the world, to those who have been blinded by the god of this world. "Let light shine out of darkness"…out of the darkness of greed, exclusion, and division that still threatens us.

As we do, keep in mind always that we do not proclaim *ourselves* –

neither as individuals, nor as churches, denominations, or religions – we proclaim, rather, Jesus Christ. And we cannot do this alone…not as individuals, nor as mere Episcopalians. We must do so together with Lutherans and Roman Catholics and other Christians as just that – Christians.

But, as Episcopalians, we like to say we believe as we pray. In a few moments, we will pray, in the words of the Nicene Creed, that "We believe in one holy catholic and apostolic church" – a unified, universal church. And in our Prayers of the People, we will pray – in the name of "the Holy One whose light shines in our world" – "for peace and unity within the church and for understanding between those of differing faiths." My prayer this World Mission Sunday is that we believe as we pray…and that we act as we believe…as Christians. The main thing is the main thing is the main thing.

AMDG

THE HOUR HAS COME
A LECTIONARY SERMON FOR LENT FIVE 2012

'The hour has come for the Son of Man to be glorified.
Very truly, I tell you, unless a grain of wheat falls into
the earth and dies, it remains just a single grain; but if
it dies, it bears much fruit. Those who love their life lose
it, and those who hate their life in this world will keep it
for eternal life. Whoever serves me must follow me, and
where I am, there will my servant be also.'[144]

Strange. We're only halfway through John's Gospel…and the "hour has come." We're at the end of Jesus' public ministry. And, next week, Palm Sunday, we begin John's long and agonizing recitation of Jesus' Passion. And, as he anticipates what is to come, Jesus, our very human brother, confesses that his "soul is troubled." But he does not flinch. He knows what he must do and what will be done to him. And, as we know, he sees it through to the end. And, as he does, he looks back – at us – and says "Follow me!"

Follow **YOU**?! To the cross? Really?!

Every year, this time of year, I'm haunted by Nikos Kazantzakis' Last Temptation of Christ, the deeply spiritual book that got the deeply spiritual Kazantzakis excommunicated from his Greek Orthodox Church. The "*last temptation*?" We have to go to the Gospel of Luke. We have to go to the cross…to the soldiers, the unrepentant criminal…the taunt "If you are the King of the Jews, save yourself!"

How easy that would have been. He was not only the King of the Jews, he was God! How easy – as in Kazantzakis' dream sequence – to climb down from the cross, to marry, raise a family, and live happily ever after on some Galilee farm...to dismiss one's followers, to renounce one's mission. But Jesus awakes from his pain-induced hallucination. He's still on the cross. He smiles. He did not shirk his duty. He did not fail. He would be that single grain that, if it dies, bears much fruit. And, smiling in that knowledge, he calls us again from the cross: "Follow me!"

As some of you know, I like to read. Another of my favorite books is one by Tim O'Brien, like me, a Vietnam veteran. It's called *The Things They Carried*.[145] I'll never forget the things *I* carried in that awful place... when, like Tim, I feared a violent death – a pack of Marlboros, a Zippo lighter, a rusty rosary my mom had snuk into my duffle bag, a picture of Mimi...and a mildewed little book – *My Imitation of Christ* by an ancient English saint, Thomas a Kempis. It was a little book that sustained me in that valley of death. Its words still sustain me, for they value not the words we speak, but the lives we live...and how we live them. "In truth," it begins, "sublime words make not a man holy and just; but a virtuous life maketh him dear to God." "I would rather feel compunction," Thomas continues, "than know its definition."[146] And what is that compunction? Much later, he writes – no, prays – "Lord Jesus, foreasmuch as thy way is narrow and despised by the world, grant that I may follow thee, and be despised by the world." "It is vanity," he says, "to wish for a long life and to take little care of leading a good life."[147]

In other words, as a Buddhist scroll in my living room puts it,

> In the end, what matters most is
> How well did you live
> How well did you love
> How well did you learn to let go.

To the extent that we are ready to let go – *of this*; to the extent that we are ready to love, we will find ourselves capable of living...living without fear...living the "good life" Thomas a Kempis and Christ would have us live.

This begs several questions. Are any of us really ready to let go...

fully…to become a grain of wheat, to fall into the earth, to die into the cosmic Christ? What then becomes of us? What is the nature of our fruit?

Consider the two German pastors I spoke of last month – Martin Niemöller and Dietrich Bonhoeffer. They both loved their God and their people and sought to save their people from the evil that had darkened their country. And, to that end, they both let go. They let go of their lives in this world – their freedom, their families, their private pleasures, and, in Bonhoeffer's case, life itself. Their fruit? They proved to Germans and to us that evil *can* be resisted. And, in doing so, they demonstrated that, among so many criminals, there were at least a few "Good Germans." By *their* imitation of Christ, they assured the survival of a remnant to rebuild the nation and to rehabilitate the badly tarnished name of the people.

Consider, of course, Martin Luther King, Jr., the anniversary of whose martyrdom we mark this year in Holy Week. Recall his final words that night before his death in Memphis. Is there any clearer statement of the meaning of this Gospel…any clearer example of letting go…than his words that night?

> Well, I don't know what will happen now. We've got some difficult days ahead. But it doesn't matter with me now. Because I've been to the mountaintop. And I don't mind. Like anybody, I would like to live a long life. Longevity has its place. But I'm not concerned about that now. I just want to do God's will. And He's allowed me to go up to the mountain. And I've looked over. And I've seen the promised land. I may not get there with you. But I want you to know tonight, that we, as a people will get to the promised land. And I'm happy, tonight. I'm not worried about anything. I'm not fearing any man. Mine eyes have seen the glory of the coming of the Lord.[148]

And Martin's fruit…his gift to us? It is the call, the goading, that, after far too many decades, we might, as a people, get to that promised land he saw – a land of real equality and economic justice.

Consider also - this morning after the anniversary of his murder thirty-two years ago - the life of Archbishop Oscar Romero of El Salvador. The son of a carpenter, who rose to prominence in an impoverished country where 40% of the land was owned by thirteen families…a country ruled by an American-supported military junta where priests and peasants who stood up for justice were routinely gunned down in cold blood.

It was only after the murder of one such priest, Rutilio Grande, however, that Romero, abandoned his previously conservative, hands-off stance. Looking at the body of his murdered friend, a Jesuit who had been organizing the *campesinos*, he said to himself: "If they have killed him for doing what he did, then I too have to walk the same path." And he did so with courage, throwing the weight of the church behind the poorest of the poor, to whom he remained simply *Monsenor*; demanding justice from the junta in San Salvador; criticizing the United States for our military aid to the US-trained generals; and drawing the ire of the Vatican.

He was standing tall and, in many ways, alone. But he was not afraid. Like all of us, he loved this life. But he was not afraid to lose it. ""Beautiful," he said, "is the moment in which we understand that we are no more than an instrument of God; we live only as long as God wants us to live; we can only do as much as God makes us able to do; we are only as intelligent as God would have us be."[149] And, two weeks before he was killed, he said: "I am bound, as a pastor, by divine command to give my life for those whom I love, and that is all Salvadorans, even those who are going to kill me."[150]

And, like Martin the night before he was martyred in Memphis, there was a wisp of premonition in *Monsenor* Romero's sermon March 23, 1980. He addressed directly those who were going to kill him, the soldiers in the pews:

> Brothers, you came from our own people. You are killing your own brothers. Any human order to kill must be subordinate to the law of God, which says, 'Thou shalt not kill'. No soldier is obliged to obey an order contrary to the

law of God. No one has to obey an immoral law. It is high time you obeyed your consciences rather than sinful orders. The church cannot remain silent before such an abomination...In the name of God, in the name of this suffering people whose cry rises to heaven more loudly each day, I implore you, I beg you, I order you: stop the repression.[151]

Next day, March 24, they answered him. That fateful day, *Monsenor* Romero entered the small chapel at the *La Divina Providencia* hospital he had long called home. The Gospel was today's – John 12:20-33. He rose... and walked to a pulpit, a lectern no more ornate than this...and spoke:

Those who surrender to the service of the poor through love of Christ, will live like the grain of wheat that dies. It only apparently dies. If it were not to die, it would remain a solitary grain. The harvest comes because of the grain that dies We know that every effort to improve society, above all when society is so full of injustice and sin, is an effort that God blesses; that God wants; that God demands of us.[152]

He finished his sermon and, as I will in just a moment, sat down. The creed was read. The prayers were said. And he strode to the altar for the Eucharist, the consecration. He held high the bread, the host. He blessed the wine and held high the cup, the words of consecration probably still echoing in his mind – "This is my Blood of the New Covenant, which is shed for you..." And, as he did, the shots rang out. The bishop, *Monsenor* Romero, fell dead behind the altar, a simple wooden table like ours, the blood, the wine, upon his chest.

He had died – no lived – into the words he had just spoken...and into the words he had spoken on an earlier occasion: "I must tell you, as a Christian, I do not believe in death without resurrection. If I am killed, I shall arise in the Salvadoran people."

Would that that was all there was to the story of *Monsenor* Romero and his people…but, sadly, no.

Five days later, 250,000 people gathered before the cathedral in San Salvador for the bishop's funeral…the largest crowd ever in Central America. A smoke bomb exploded. Two or three more. And, then, the snipers in civilian clothes started firing into the crowd from the roof of the National Assembly building. When it was over, more than thirty people lay dead on the square and countless more wounded. And in the months and years that followed, the death squads under the notorious Major D'Aubisson wreaked havoc on the nation, killing 60,000, sending countless thousands fleeing the country in search of safety. Many thousands came to the United States. And many are still with us here in Contra Costa… contributing to our economy but forced still to live in the shadows.

We had sinned twice in El Salvador. We had armed the killers. And we had denied their victims asylum.

And, in 1981, I found myself drawn into the efforts to right those wrongs. In the midst of a tour of duty at the Carnegie Endowment for International Peace, I found myself in the office next to that of Bob White, our just returned Ambassador to El Salvador. I listened to his heartfelt testimony and joined him in spreading the sordid truth around Washington about our role in El Salvador.

We were joined in those efforts by Bianca Jagger, the singer's Nicaraguan-born ex-wife. An actress, model, and jet-setter, she had just returned from a Congressional trip to Honduras and a life-changing confrontation with a Salvadoran death squad on that country's border with El Salvador. She has since devoted her life to the cause of human rights from Africa to Afghanistan and now serves on the board of Amnesty International.

In 1981 in downtown Washington, however, she and Bob White went from church to church telling their stories and urging the churches, begging them to establish basement sanctuaries for the Salvadoran – and Guatemalan – refugees just beginning to drift in. And I was privileged to accompany them and help as I could…if only to make the coffee.

And the next year – thirty years ago this weekend, the New Sanctuary Movement was begun in Tucson by John Fife.

In a sense, Oscar Romero was resurrected not only in the Salvadoran people, but in Bob, Bianca, John…and, I expect, in many of you. I feel his spirit *right now*…urging us to serve, to follow, to water the seeds that have been sown, to plant our own – not by dying, but by living…fearlessly, intentionally.

These saints - Dietrich Bonhoeffer, Martin Luther King, Jr., and Oscar Romero - are among the ten martyrs of the twentieth century who are carved in stone above Westminster Abbey's Great West Door – icons to be sure and surely worth looking up too. But I can't think of them as stone figures frozen in time. For they were living, breathing human beings, whose lives, however tangentially, touched mine…and, I hope, yours. They live still…*in* us…as does Christ. And, they are speaking still…as is Christ: "Whoever serves me must follow me, and where I am, there will my servant be also."

Follow *YOU*?! To the cross? Really?! **Really**?

AMDG

NOT A NEEDY ONE AMONG THEM
A LECTIONARY SERMON FOR EASTER TWO 2012

There was not a needy person among them, for as many as owned lands or houses sold them and brought the proceeds of what was sold. They laid it at the apostles' feet, and it was distributed to each as any had need. [153]

Seems to me this is the third or fourth year in a row that I've preached this Sunday after Easter…the vicar's well-deserved Sabbath. Seems to me also that I've exhausted all I know – and probably all you want to hear - about Thomas and his doubts. So let me turn to Acts…to the once…and, I pray, future church.

But, first, a reminder…about the date. Do we really need one? We all know what April 15 means – pay the man…give to Caesar what is Caesar's.

And how much might that be? What's fair? What's necessary? 10%? 15%? Twenty? Thirty-five? And, when it's all raked in by our various caesars – our local, state, and federal governments – what is it spent on? Tanks? Bombers? Prisons? Subsidies for oil companies? Tax cuts for billionaires? Or is it spent on schools, hospitals, libraries, feeding hungry children, healing wounded veterans? Budgets, as Mother Susan has reminded us, are moral documents.

What's left for church? Five percent? Seven? Ten? And how's that spent? The upkeep of aging buildings? Replacing fine silken vestments? Travel to conferences and conventions? Lawyers to retrieve property from breakaway parishes? Or feeding the hungry and healing all the wounded among us?

And, after we've shelled out our ten, twenty or thirty percent to God *and* Caesar, to church and state, what's left for us? As Americans, plenty! But, as we've become all too aware these past few years, too many of our brothers and sisters are in need and suffering in this land of plenty. Right and left, we're bombarded by appeals to respond. What are we to do?

Simple, we're told today. Sell your house. Sell your land...*all of it.* Take the proceeds and distribute it to each as any has need. And, not to worry, the community will take care of your needs in the same way. We'll put mattresses on the benches along the sides. You can sleep here. We all can.

And that's indeed the way it was done in the first Christian community in Jerusalem. As we're told here and earlier in Acts "everything they owned was held in common" and they "spent much time together in the temple... broke bread at home and ate their food with glad and generous hearts."[154] It was a golden age, a Camelot of sorts...a place in time from which we've strayed so very, very far...a time and place, like Camelot, that has faded in the mists of what was, what might have been, and, I pray, might yet be once again. It was an ideal – Christ's ideal – an ideal that seems no longer to have a place in hearts hardened by fear and greed, in minds clouded by irony, cynicism, and complacency.

How far have we strayed from that ideal – that brief, shining moment in Easter's aftermath in first-century Jerusalem? I was reminded just how far as I read last Sunday's papers. In the *New York Times*, I read in the business section about the annual income of Apple's new CEO - $378 million...or $4,536 a second. And, on the front page, I read of many thousands of poor people losing their meager cash assistance in the name of "welfare reform" and the single mothers among them, desperate to make ends meet, who "have sold food stamps, sold blood, skipped meals, shoplifted, doubled up with friends, scavenged trash bins for bottles and cans and returned to relationships with violent partners — all with children in tow."

Still, the critics – professed Christians among them – prefer this current American reality to the apostles' version of the Beloved Community...a community, they insist, that smacked of socialism. "*We're* capitalists," they tell us, "let the 'Market' take care of things"…the cold, invisible, amoral "Hand of the Market"…with which we would wash our hands of moral choice and in the name of which we would absolve ourselves of any sin.

But they're wrong. They're wrong on three counts.

Yes, we are capitalists. There's nothing inherently wrong about that… and there's much that is commendable. But, for the last century and certainly since the Great Depression, ours has not been the sort of vulture capitalism that held sway in the first Gilded Age and that threatens again. No, ours has been a limited capitalism in which the amoral "Invisible Hand of the Market" has been restrained by prudent regulation and in which the excesses of Social Darwinism have been checked by compassion.

And, no, the apostles' ideal community did not smack of socialism – neither European social democracy - which is but a form of limited capitalism - nor the murderous state socialism of Stalinist Russia. It more closely resembled – Take a deep breath! – communism…the ideal community propounded by Karl Marx. According to Marx, the ideal communist community would follow the withering away of the state and all forms of coercion. Communism, he wrote, would "deprive no man of the ability to appropriate the fruits of his labor. The only thing it [would] deprive him of is the ability to enslave others by means of such appropriations." Goods would be distributed "from each, according to his ability; to each, according to his needs."

I wonder where he got *that* idea? Once again, I can hear the voice of that "Church Lady" from Saturday Night Live" – "Would you believe *JESUS*?!"

I'm reminded in this regard of something once said by "Che" Guevara, "San Ernesto" to folks in Bolivia. "The true revolutionary," he said, "is guided by great feelings of love. It is impossible to think of a genuine revolutionary lacking this quality….There is no other definition of communism valid for us than that of the abolition of the exploitation of man by man." And, I must ask: Is there any truer revolutionary than Jesus?

Was there any greater love than his? Did he not die for love of us? Did he not preach the abolition of the exploitation of man by man? Are we not called to practice that same love? Are we not called to seek that same goal?

And, it is in regard to this, our calling, that the cynical critics of the apostles' Beloved Community are most wrong. We cannot, as Christians, surrender the exercise of our moral agency to mechanistic pseudo-gods such as Adam Smith's "Invisible Hand." We cannot agree with Karl Marx that man is nothing more than an economic animal. Nor can we agree with Ayn Rand that economic self-interest is all that should motivate us. We have a long line of martyrs from Stephen to Martin who have demonstrated that man does not live by bread alone nor die for self alone.

So, as we face the harsh realities of this American Spring, what are we expected to make of this passage from Acts? What are we to do with it?

Might we begin by deconstructing its message, breaking it down into digestible bite-size pieces?

First, recognize that it describes an ideal – an ideal only imperfectly approximated by today's monastic communities…an ideal only achievable even by the apostles, thanks to their first-hand experience of the Resurrection and Pentecost. As we're told in the preceding verse, they were immediate experiences that left them shaken and filled with the Holy Spirit. They were moved and empowered in ways *we* can only imagine.

Second, there was an over-riding purpose to their living together and sharing. They wanted to ensure that no one among them was in any need.

Third, there was a unity to all that they did – a unity that eludes our fractured churches today – for they were all "of one heart and soul." They were not weighed down by dry rituals, rules, and regulations, nor distracted by theological "gotcha" games. They were, rather, fired up and propelled forward by love. They understood, as perhaps never since, that the main thing is the main thing is the main thing.

Fourth, unlike the closed, inward looking monasteries that, by their nature, must fall short of this first century ideal, the apostles understood that theirs was an outward looking mission – to give "testimony to the

Resurrection of the Lord"…testimony best conveyed to others by demonstrating their love for each by how they lived. And, thanks to the "great power" with which they carried out this mission, the community grew, as "day by day the Lord added to their number those who were being saved."[155]

Is there some way, then, that we can reassemble these pieces into some new manageable whole from whence we can seek to retrieve this lost ideal? I think we can.

First, we have to shake off the paralysis and despair that stems from the seemingly daunting nature of the task. Rome was not built in a day and neither will the Kingdom of God. And we don't have to move into the sanctuary together to get started. We've already started in ways we might not recognize. Consider that Agape supper Thursday before last. Consider our covenant groups. Haven't we, too, "spent much time together in the temple…broken bread at home and ate…food with glad and generous hearts." Might we not seek to tap more deeply into the power of the Resurrection and Pentecost – a power diluted perhaps by the distance of two thousand years – by spending more time in Bible study and prayer together…as we've already begun?

Second, we need to be more intentional about alleviating poverty. That was the central theme of Jesus' ministry and must be of ours. In this regard, our Association of Episcopal Deacons is proposing a General Convention resolution urging us to begin every church meeting – at whatever level, of whatever nature – with a discussion of and reflection on what we are doing alleviate poverty. All well and good. I hope it passes. I hope we have those discussions. But you know me. Talk is cheap. We have to move beyond talk. What are we going to *do* about it? And I don't mean just write a check. If we're going to empower the poor – empower ourselves – we have to experience each other. We have to *see* the poor and touch them…and they must see us and touch us. The question was not "to whom do we write the check," but "when was it that we saw you hungry and gave you food….or naked and gave you clothing." If we don't look, how can we see the face of Christ in the other.

And, again, don't be paralyzed by the ideal. Don't let the absence of the perfect crowd out the good. We don't have to sell our homes and dump the proceeds in the narthex. But we must do **something** when we confront poverty. To quote Nkosi Johnson, a South African boy dying of AIDS, "We must do the best we can with what we have in the time we have."

I was baptized in a church bearing the name of Saint Martin of Tours, a Roman soldier. His story is worth recalling. One cold night he met a freezing beggar. Not having any money, he cut his cloak in half and gave half to the beggar. That night Jesus appeared to him in a dream, wearing half a cloak. Next morning, he sought Baptism.

Do such things happen today? Yes…they do. Last Monday, we had a death in our Open Cathedral congregation, an apparent suicide, and this afternoon we'll celebrate Nae Nae's short, troubled life under a beautiful blue sky. But, Tuesday night our Open Cathedral community – our family – huddled together in an upstairs room in the Tenderloin to grieve. Among us was Nae Nae's fiancé, Marquis, who had lost his meager financial assistance and just been evicted from his SRO room. In his grief, he faced a cold and rainy night on the street. One of our number, Ion, partially blind and developmentally disabled, offered Marquis half his disability check. Later, as we were eating, two latecomers joined us. There was no more food. But the others – hungry and homeless themselves – shared the food from their plates. On the drive home, I turned up the volume on Bruce Springsteen's latest – "We Take Care of Our Own."

Consider, then, the third element of today's message – unity! If we are going to take care of our own – and, all God's poor are our own – then we have to hang together in solidarity…not just in our bickering Episcopal Church and Anglican Communion, but also with **all** Christians, and all those of other faiths and none who would work with us to build the Beloved Community. The main thing is the main thing is the main thing…and it is love.

Finally, as we've already undertaken here at Christ the Lord, we have to share Christ's love and ***our*** own with our broader community that is Pinole, Contra Costa, and the world. As was the apostles', ours must be an outward looking – outward ***doing*** - mission.

It's not a mission that can be accomplished overnight. It's not one that can be accomplished in our lifetimes. But we must take the first steps in the hope and with confidence that some future generation will say of us "They took care of their own…There was not a needy person among them."

AMDG

GOD ON THE MOVE
A LECTIONARY SERMON FOR PENTECOST EIGHT 2012

I have not lived in a house since the day I brought up the people of Israel from Egypt to this day, but I have been moving about in a tent and a tabernacle [156]

My, it's good to be home…to relax in my garden, to sleep in my own bed, to hug Cocoa, and, once again, to be with you.

Indianapolis, mind you, is not without its charms, particularly if you're a sports fan – a football stadium, a baseball field, and a basketball arena all within two blocks of the hotel; a spectacular fireworks display on the Fourth; a personal pilgrimage to the Kurt Vonnegut Museum; and quiet time – alone – in Christ Church Cathedral.

And there were more than a few joys – the chance to renew acquaintances with old friends and to make new ones, that afternoon in the House of Bishops when all the ministries of the church were opened to transgendered Episcopalians, Bishop Marc's key role in bringing that about, the celebratory Integrity Eucharist that evening, Teal's Baptism at the TransEpiscopal Eucharist two days later, that afternoon in the House of Deputies when the church adopted a provisional liturgy for the blessing of lifelong same-gender relationships, and the bitter-sweet opportunity in that house to speak my mind on Palestine.

But there were also challenges, not the least of which was the weather – the hottest day in 75 years…and a week to match. This mid-convention headline – 105 – is not something to be laughed at or a passing phenomenon. It has been accompanied by a severe drought and the corn is only waist high. Our sisters and brothers in the heartland need our prayers for rain. This aging body also felt the strain of day-in/day-out fifteen-hour days and missed meals…cough drops for lunch, and, more than once, peanuts or cheese and crackers for dinner. And it was less than pleasant to watch the church's sausage being made and to have to struggle with the defenders of the status quo for control of the meat grinder.

If all this sounds unappetizing, it should, for it was. And, if it doesn't sound much like church, there's no reason it should, for it wasn't…not for the most part, not by my lights. The proceedings – particularly about structure and budget – reminded me much more of the power politics I had experienced in government, often without the diplomatic niceties that marked my years in the State Department.

Maybe I was too close to the meat grinder; I never kidded myself into thinking I had any control of the handle, but could see quite clearly who did. Maybe I was too deeply entwined in the forest of our deputation or the work of the legislative committees to see a clear way out to pasture and peace. Maybe I was too personally involved on two key issues – Palestine and transgender inclusion – to view the process with the same equanimity as others.

Whatever the reasons, I found myself – already the week before convention – physically exhausted and emotionally drained and, in its wake – and still - struggling through a spiritual crisis of sorts, wondering what to make of an institution that, far from confronting the powers-that-be, seems to have been infiltrated by them.

In a personal and sharply focused way, that was driven home on the issue of Palestine. In her Sunday morning sermon, the Presiding Bishop challenged us to "Tell it like it really is." So, let me do so. I was appalled by the way she and her staff intervened to gut even the mildest resolution of even any mention of the Palestinian Christians' cry for justice - their 2009 Kairos Document; to silence those who urged that it be read or – heaven forbid - acted upon; and to substitute a vacuous, over-long resolution that amounted to neutrality and silence in the face of injustice… this despite testimonies from dozens of Christians and Jews and a personal message from Desmond Tutu pleading for action. It was an unfortunate resolution and it and a similarly anodyne companion resolution generated an unusual minority report. Together, they were called "gutless" by another bishop on the committee and gave me an opportunity to address the elephant in the room – the canard of anti-Semitism – on the floor of the House of Deputies. I did. No one else spoke up. End of debate.

But, even more spiritually troubling to anyone who cares about the health of the Church, was the far larger debate surrounding the shape and direction of this human institution we call the Episcopal Church – what the Church, as assembled in Indianapolis, calls PB&F or Programs, Budget, and Finances.

In the face of a dwindling, aging membership, the debate focused not so much on content or mission, as on the levers of power and the shape of the institution…on whether church leadership would be consolidated into the hands of the Presiding Bishop and her staff or continue to be shared – with greater transparency – between the two houses of bishops and deputies. Would power be concentrated more greatly in that edifice known as "815" in New York? Or would power be devolved outward, downward to dioceses, parishes, offices around the country? 815, itself, became the icon in a lively debate about the institution we call church, with one deputy quipping "Constantine has left the building…and he left it to us." And, after the House of Deputies decided to sell the building – a move later "indefinitely postponed" by the House of Bishops - a youth delegate from Kansas asked me "Where would they move if they sell it?" I replied "Perhaps a garage in Wichita."

All this back-and-forth about money and power and buildings was starting to get to me. I no longer found it very humorous. Where was the Spirit? Where was the response to young people – and more than a few old people - looking for content, looking for relevance? Where was the response to Maryanne, the youth delegate who blogged:

> Today's struggle for me has been to remain present in this convention, as I have become more convinced than ever

that Church is not something that happens within four walls (and especially not something that happens within four non-unionized hotels).

Back in my hotel room, I pulled the Bible from the night table draw and found myself reading about the God we heard about this morning, a God on the move, a God who has no need for a building – *any* building, a God who tells the prophet Nathan: "I have not lived in a house since the day I brought up the people of Israel from Egypt to this day, but I have been moving about in a tent and a tabernacle." Flipping forward to the New Testament, I found a parallel in Jesus – same God, different form - always on the move, never stopping, preaching on the way...on a hillside, in a village square, on the shore beside a boat. "Foxes have holes, and birds of the air have nests," he tells us, "but the Son of Man has nowhere to lay his head." And, he turns to us, and says "Follow me!"

In my reflection, I turned to a pre-convention blog by Richard Helmer, a priest and member of our deputation. "Then why have an institution at all?" he asked.

> Is it preferable to shed the shells and tatty clothes of the institution and return to the dusty roads the first disciples walked, where "The Son of Man has nowhere to lay his head"? It's a romantic notion of Church, to be sure, but is it as real or as tangible as the challenges we face these days with a fleet of buildings and organizations and a faithful band of pilgrims that need careful and attentive stewarding through the storms of both today and tomorrow?

> Another way sees the institution as the Church writ large, with all of its powers, walls, and boundaries clearly delineated and illuminated by doctrine, tradition, and practice. The danger of this thinking is that the institution's mission too easily becomes self-serving. The Church as

institution becomes its own glorious, but more often ignominious end. The mission becomes rebuilding and preserving the institution as we see it, which is little better than mere survival.[157]

After a few days in the heat of Indianapolis and another night of heated debate, I found him blogging again and I found myself sharing the frustration of his dilemma"

I came to General Convention ready to "blow things up and start over." In a world of floundering and often inept institutions, re-starts seem to be the only way forward. So I was anxious to attend the church structure hearing on Thursday night, expecting a host of brilliant ideas and strategies to come from the grassroots of our Church; hoping to come away with a sense that we have the raw material to build a new, nimble institution from the rubble of a sclerotic corporate structure that is a throwback to the 1950's.

After listening to an hour-and-a-half of impassioned testimony, however, I came away more puzzled than heartened. I heard a great deal of high philosophical talk and theologizing and spiritualizing assertion, but no memorable substance for the direction we ought to take in re-organizing our Church. The most helpful remark of the evening for me was a deputy pointing out that we are now in that no-man's land between knowing we need to change but not knowing how we ought to change.[158]

In typical Episcopalian fashion, when finding ourselves in such a place, the convention punted, creating a task force to "re-imagine" the Church.

We are still in that no-man's land. The crisis continues. But the opportunity inherent in any crisis lies before us…beckoning. Not to worry, God declares to Nathan, "the Lord will make you a house." "I will," he says, "establish his kingdom" and, then, and only then, will the Lord "build a house for my name, and I will establish the throne of his kingdom forever."[159] What sort of kingdom? What sort of house? In the reading we didn't hear this morning, Paul tells the Ephesians God will build us a house "built upon the foundation of the apostles and prophets, with Christ Jesus himself as the cornerstone." "In him," he says, "the whole structure is joined together and grows into a holy temple in the Lord; in whom you also are built together spiritually into a dwelling-place for God."[160]

Yes, when we get there, there *will* be a temple, a house built not of bricks and mortar, but of flesh and blood and spirit. To paraphrase Pogo, we will have found our home and it will be us.

In the meantime, Christ has shown us the way to that Promised Land. He has, as Paul told the Ephesians, "broken down the dividing wall, that is, the hostility between us."[161] No longer are we Jews and Gentiles, strangers and aliens. We are all one people-of-God, sojourners on the same journey. Listen to Bonnie Anderson, our outgoing President of the House of Deputies, champion of the laity, and an outspoken "troublemaker" *par excellence*:

> Let's be honest. We in the Episcopal Church have been forced to get on the road toward the Promised Land. Some of us are happy about that, because being the institutional church of power and privilege, which we used to be, seemed a lot like being slaves in Egypt. Others of us were doing just fine in Egypt, and we'd be happier going back there. We're wandering in a wilderness of declining membership and budget reductions and we're pretty sure that we're going to die out here.
>
> But there's no going back to Egypt. We're on the Promised

Land highway, and we're spending a lot of time acting like the Israelites. We whine, we don't trust each other, and we try to hoard what we have been given even though it won't keep. Even though when we take more than we need, it breeds worms and becomes foul. And I'm pretty sure that we can all name some golden calves that we've been worshiping.

We need to cut it out. All of us. If we're going to reach the Promised Land together, in one piece, we need the God-given gifts of everyone who's on this journey.[162]

As we hold hands and prepare to take our next first step together, let me suggest two more guides for the journey – Francis and John.

It was nine hundred years ago when Francis heard God speak in that crumbling church of San Damiano - "Francis, don't you see that my house is being destroyed? Go then and rebuild it for me." Only slowly did Francis realize that God meant not the earthquake ravaged building, but rather the Church-writ-large of God's suffering people who were then being led astray by venial, hypocritical shepherds who had succumbed to the powers-that-be. And he did rebuild the church by witnessing to the truth of the Gospel. In the midst of a post-Christian culture marked by materialism and greed, are we not being called again to rebuild a sometimes gutless Church, a Church again grown corpulent and comfortable?

And, have we not been called to re-imagine the nature of the Church we seek to build? Can we not imagine a Church not of buildings and walls, bricks and mortar, mortgages and debts, but rather of God's people praying together, singing together in Fernandez Park, in United Nations Plaza, or at a BART station in the Mission, or a Home Depot parking lot in El Cerrito? Is it really just "a romantic notion" to "shed the shells and tatty clothes of the institution and return to the dusty roads the first disciples walked, where 'The Son of Man has nowhere to lay his head'"? Is Bonnie just a dreamer to envisage a "people-of-God church, united in our shared leadership and the love and liberation of Jesus Christ"?

I've sometimes been called "strident" or "provocative." I was in Indianapolis. And some have called me too romantic…or, more than once, a dreamer. But I find I'm in good company…which brings me back to John:

> Imagine no possessions
> I wonder if you can
> No need for greed or hunger
> A brotherhood of man
> Imagine all the people sharing all the world
>
> You, you may say
> I'm a dreamer, but I'm not the only one
> I hope some day you'll join us
> And the world will live as one[163]

AMDG

WHO IS WISDOM? WHAT IS WISDOM?
A LECTIONARY SERMON FOR PENTECOST SIXTEEN
2012

Wisdom cries out in the street;
In the squares she raises her voice.[164]

I've been given wide latitude by you and Mother Susan to preach the truth as I understand it. I'm blessed by that and I'm grateful.

There have, however, been two occasions when I was asked to tone it down...to mind my "P"s and "Q"s. Most recently – a couple of weeks ago – one parishioner suggested that I stop talking so much about women. "Make some room for men. This is a Christian church and Christ was a man."

So...let me talk about a woman...and speculate about God as woman. The woman? Her name is Sophia. That's Greek for Wisdom. And, in ***their*** wisdom, our lectionary writers have given us an opportunity this month – a challenge - to consider Sophia and an aspect of God we Christians hardly ever touch...to ask "Who is Wisdom? What is wisdom?" But, even in the snippets from Proverbs and the Wisdom of Solomon they have chosen for us, we tip toe around the questions they raise, the mystery they point to about the feminine side of a genderless God. They cause us discomfort. They cause us to squirm. "Where is this Wisdom in the Creed?" some ask. "How can there be a fourth face to a Trinity?" Still others look at the person in my position and perhaps complain "You're supposed to give us answers, not raise questions."

Oh?! You don't really want me to do your thinking for you, do you? Don't we Episcopalians pride ourselves on not parking our minds at the door when we enter church each Sunday? Would you – should you – believe

anyone who tells you that they ***know*** what God looks like. Is there not a difference between knowing and belief? Is there not a reason we are called believers?

So, taking advantage of the latitude you've given me, let me tell you what I believe about Wisdom and about God...not what I ***know***, but what I ***believe***.

Let's begin at the Beginning...and maybe a bit before. In the Beginning, Genesis tells us, "God created humankind in his image, in the image of God he created them; male and female he created them."[165] The Creation story is, as we know, metaphor. But, even as metaphor, these words clearly convey the image of a Creator God who is both male and female, both mother and father...the Creator God I invoke at the start of my every sermon.

Then there is the even more profound mystery of what the empty void was like ***before*** Creation. What was God was like in the darkness before there was light; in that emptiness, that infinitely tiny, infinitely dense nucleus before the "Big Bang;" in that singular loneliness before our creation or the creation of even a bird or fish or plant...or speck of cosmic dust? I remember reading once of a wise rabbi who would warn his students "Don't go there!" Only the most courageous soul would consider doing so. It's dangerous territory. But the writers of Proverbs beckon us to peek behind the veil of creation – to a still earlier time – to ponder the feminine image of Wisdom who says in Proverbs 8

> The LORD created me at the beginning of his work, the first of his acts of long ago. Ages ago I was set up, at the first, before the beginning of the earth. When there were no depths I was brought forth, when there were no springs abounding with water ...When he marked out the foundations of the earth, then I was beside him, like a master worker; and I was daily his delight, rejoicing before him always.[166]

Here we have the image of a partner, a co-worker, a delightful helpmate for a perhaps lonely God. But, as Andrew Seeley of Thomas Aquinas College points out, she cannot *be* God if she was "created"…not any more than we or the angels or any other created being can be.[167] And, if only a metaphor, how appropriate that it is of a delightful feminine helpmate. For the Book of Proverbs was written primarily for young Jewish men coming of age. It seeks not only to *describe* Wisdom, but to *impart* wisdom …to instruct them on how to live one's life and how best to gain the attention of a young man than to speak to him with the soft voice of a woman? I recall how, in Navy fighter jets of my youth, an emergency situation was announced to the then-almost always male pilot in a soft female voice – as in "Your right wing has just fallen off."

But, what if Wisdom, who speaks to us also in the Wisdom of Solomon and Sirach, Ecclesiastes, and Job, is more than just a male-concocted metaphor. Might this, indeed, be the feminine voice of God? Perhaps… if we speak of Wisdom not as being "created" but "brought forth," another formulation used in the Proverbs passage I just read. For his part, Seeley turns to the Wisdom of Solomon…to the verse just preceding our reading this morning. She is, it says, "a breath of the power of God and a pure emanation of the glory of the Almighty"[168]…reflecting, as we just heard, "the eternal light of God's deeds and goodness." *This* Wisdom is not created from nothing, but is emanated or spun off from God…"begotten not made…light from light." Sound familiar? Sound more comfortable?

Consider also these familiar opening lines from John…and a final speculation:

> In the beginning was the Word, and the Word was with God, and the Word was God. He was in the beginning with God. All things came into being through him, and without him not one thing came into being. What has come into being in him was life, and the life was the light of all people. The light shines in the darkness, and the

darkness did not overcome it.[169]

The speculation? Might this Divine Word, this Logos, be Wisdom? Might Wisdom be Jesus? Was not Wisdom "in the beginning with God?" Does she not reflect the eternal light that shines in the darkness and weren't we told this morning that "she cannot be changed by the power of evil"… cannot be overcome by darkness?

I don't take every word literally, but I do believe in the power and integrity of words and, again and again, turn to my college dictionary to seek clarity about their meaning. Here's how that dictionary defines "logos:" It is "the rational principle that governs and develops the universe." Again, sound familiar? It should. Does not the Wisdom of Solomon tell us Wisdom "orders all things well?"[170]

I'll leave it at that…the speculation. I won't deign to do your thinking for you. Instead, I urge you to read these Wisdom books, to draw your own conclusions, and to seek Wisdom who "is more beautiful than the sun and stars." As you do, I urge you to engage both mind and heart, for wisdom is found only by the combined effort of both.

But getting to know God better – be it in Wisdom or Jesus – is only half of what we are called to as Christians. The other half is to discern what God wants us to do in our life, with our life…and to carry out on earth as it is in heaven the will of God as best we understand it.

Let me turn, then, to what our readings today have to say to us on that score. That, unfortunately, takes me to the second of the objections to my preaching…one raised over an early spring coffee hour by another parishioner who turned to me with a look of exasperation and said "If there's one thing I don't need to hear any more about, it's Occupy."

Fact is, I've said very little about Occupy since then…not because I disagreed with its goals or because I trim my sails easily, but because events conspired to remove the movement from day-to-day public consciousness. The coordinated police crackdown had worked its way. The camps were broken up and the demonstrations increasingly less tolerated. Internally, the energy was sapped by the dysfunctional nature of a leaderless movement dependent on total consensus. And, unlike its role in earlier civil rights and peace movements, the church sat by in silent disinterest as young people cried out in the streets for economic fairness and social justice.

Yes, I've said very little about Occupy over the summer. But today's readings and tomorrow's anniversary suggest this might be a good time to do so again.

It was a year ago tomorrow that ordinary people gathered around that snorting bronze bull – that Golden Calf - in New York's Financial District and cried "Enough!"…Enough of the soulless, uncaring greed; the trampling on the weak; the ever-widening chasm between rich and poor, between the one-tenth of one percent and the ninety-nine percent; the distortion of democracy by money; the mockery of a government bought and paid for by seven banks "too big to fail." The crowd swelled…and they marched…past a silent Trinity Church…to Zuccott Park, a now-privatized public space in the absent shadow of the World Trade Center. And, soon enough, the little tents went up…in Zuccotti Park, in Oakland's Frank Ogawa Plaza, in San Francisco's Justin Herman Plaza, and in countless other cities as the people reclaimed the commons.

And the people marched…and cried out in the streets, because their voices had too long gone unheard in our corporate media or in the ballot box. There was a wisdom in the signs we carried…a simple folk wisdom. "I'll believe corporations are people, when Texas executes one," one read. Another proclaimed "We're not camping. We're exercising our first amendment rights." A favorite of mine said "Obama is not a brown-skinned anti-war socialist who gives away free healthcare…You're thinking of Jesus."

How clearly it all came back, as I reflected this week on our reading from Proverbs:

> Wisdom cries out in the street;
>> in the squares she raises her voice.
> At the busiest corner she cries out;
>> at the entrance of the city gates she speaks:

'How long, O simple ones, will you love being simple?
How long will scoffers delight in their scoffing
and fools hate knowledge?
For waywardness kills the simple,
and the complacency of fools destroys them.[171]

We had thrown off our complacency. We had raised our voices. And, tomorrow we will again cry out at the "busiest corner" – at California and Kearney in San Francisco. And those of us who *do* think of Jesus will again pose his question to the one percent… and all who seek not God, but gold – "What will it profit them to gain the whole world and forfeit their life?"

And, in the quiet that follows the noise, we will ask the other questions that are begged: How much is enough? How much is too much… or not enough? How do we close the gap? How do we create a society in which there is not a one percent or ninety-nine, but rather one hundred percent who live together in the harmony and abundance that's called Shalom? How do we achieve the balance sought in Proverbs by Agur son of Jakeh who prays to God for *just enough*, lest he lose his life…his eternal life?

…give me neither poverty nor riches; feed me with
the food that I need, or I shall be full, and deny you,
and say, 'Who is the LORD?' or I shall be poor, and
steal, and profane the name of my God.[172]

Last weekend, at the funeral for a dear friend, I heard some words that comport with Agur's prayer and suggest some answers to the questions we will pose tomorrow at California and Kearney and that Jesus posed in Caesarea Phillippi to his would-be followers. As if to put down that ugly bumper sticker – "He who dies with the most toys wins" – Ralph Waldo Emerson wrote, that, to the contrary,

To leave the world a bit better, whether by a healthy
child, a garden patch, or a redeemed social condition;
To know even one life has breathed easier because
you have lived. This is to have succeeded.[173]

It is how we are to live, if we are to save our lives. It is, when all is said and done, the beginning of wisdom.

AMDG

WHAT IS CAESAR'S? WHAT IS MINE? WHAT IS GOD'S? A LECTIONARY SERMON FOR PENTECOST EIGHTEEN 2012

***Render unto Caesar the things which are Caesar's
and unto God the things that are God's***[174]

That, of course, is the traditional version of Jesus' ambiguous reply to the Pharisees' "gotcha" question we just heard – "Is it lawful to pay taxes to the emperor or not?"

Damned if you do. Damned if you don't. If he answered "No," he'd be hauled before Herod and the Romans on charges of treason. And the penalty for not paying taxes to the Romans was death. If he answered "Yes," he'd be hauled before the Sanhedrin on charges of heresy.

And this question of taxes was no small matter in Jesus' time, especially in Galilee. It wasn't just a Tea Party threat – "No new taxes or we'll vote for the other candidate." No, there was rebellion in the air…like pepper spray on Wall Street. Jewish nationalists of the day were opposed not only to no ***new*** taxes, but to ***any*** taxes. And, just thirty years later, another Galilean named Judas founded a sect called the Zealots and incited his countrymen to revolt, declaring, the historian Josephus tells us, "that they were cowards if they submitted to paying taxes to the Romans after serving God alone."[175] And we all know how that ended – mass suicide at Masada and the destruction of the Temple in Jerusalem!

Jesus was well aware of the tension in the air and the volatile nature of this question of taxes. He chose his words carefully – not so much to teach, as to avoid another of the many traps the Pharisees were always setting for him. In that sense, this story should be seen not so much as an example of Jesus' teaching, but as an example of his ability to think on his feet.

The resultant ambiguity comes down to us across the millennia in the haunting question – "What is Caesar's, what is mine, and what is God's in this temporal life?" And, in that question, we've been presented a valuable teaching tool that New Testament scholars have used in much the same way rabbis do in seeking meaning from the Torah. They've used it here as a *midrash* – on the one hand, on the other – to tease out the day-to-day situational ethics of how to balance our loyalties to God and to government and all the temporal powers that be. What is properly our share of what we earn? What is the government's? What is society's? What is God's? What is a fair share?

Last Sunday we celebrated Francis. If we followed his example, we'd give it **all** to God. Not a bad message as we kick-off our stewardship campaign.

Mind you, Francis was not always so altruistic. Indeed, in his youth, he was something of a roustabout and spendthrift. Then one day, kneeling before the altar in his parish church, he heard a voice - "Francis, repair my church. Assuming this meant church with a small "c," he took some fabric from his father's shop and sold it to get money to repair the crumbling walls of his parish church. Outraged, his father Pietro dragged Francis before the bishop and, in front of the whole town, demanded that Francis return the money and renounce all rights as his heir.

The kindly bishop told him to return the money, telling him God would provide. Delighted, Francis not only gave back the money but stripped off all his clothes -- the clothes his father had given him. Standing before the crowd, stark naked, he said, "Pietro Bernardone is no longer my father. From now on I can say with complete freedom, 'Our Father who art in heaven.'" Wearing nothing but castoff rags, he went off into the freezing woods - singing. From then on Francis had nothing...and everything. And he went on to repair the church that has no walls.

Not to worry. I'm not going to ask you to strip down and lay your clothes before the altar. I'm not going to ask you to give your last penny to God or to the church...much as such an example might serve to inspire a church writ large that is again so much in need to repair.

No, I recognize that we are all human beings who must tend to body as well as soul. We must put aside some of what we earn to feed ourselves, to provide housing for our families, their health care, and, yes, some of the little things of life that give us joy – new shoes, a good book, a night out. I recognize, too, that, in these hard times, it is hard to find the wherewithal to do even that.

Against that background, too many of us are inclined to insist there's no need to share with God *or* government. It's mine. I earned it. I'll keep it – all of it!

Which brings us back to where we started – to taxes – and that gotcha question: "Is it lawful to pay taxes to the emperor or not?" To the "emperors" in Washington, Sacramento, and Pinole? It's a question Jesus had to deal with. And so do we…as individuals and as a church.

And, speaking of church, there was, in Jesus' day, a rather steep Temple tax on top of the Emperor's tax. How steep? Would you believe 21 percent? And the Jews couldn't pay it with the coin – the denarius – Jesus held up in this story. For, on one side of the coin was a picture of Augustus, and, on the other, the likeness of Tiberius and an inscription declaring him a god. To use such a coin to pay the Temple tax or buy a sacrificial dove or animal would be blasphemy. It was dirty money. Enter the money launderers, the money changers in the Temple courtyard who took their cut in much the way we pay an exchange fee at a foreign airport or an ever increasing ATM fee each time we use our debit card.

The church today has no such problem. We'll gladly accept your coins and dollars – any denomination – with no exchange fee. To be sure, with the short-lived exception of the Susan B. Anthony, they're all coins and bills bearing the image of some dead white man. But they all remind us on the other side that it is "In God we trust."

And, like Jesus' denarii, it is lawful to pay our taxes to our governments with those same dollars. That's why they're called *legal* tender. But, is it morally right and good to do so? What do we get for our money? Is it worth what we pay?

Oliver Wendell Holmes's said that "Taxes are what we pay for civilized society."[176] And didn't even the Romans provide a civilized society – running water, good roads, the peace of *Pax Romana*? And how much worthier is our government, a government, not imposed, but formed **by us** to "establish justice, insure domestic tranquility, provide for the common defense, promote the general welfare, and secure the blessings of liberty to ourselves and our posterity…." Aren't these *moral* goods? Aren't they the underpinning of the peace of *Shalom*?

Like the late Tony Judt[177], I fear that we've lost this sense of common purpose, common good, common wealth. After decades of greed and now in a time of scarcity and insecurity, we're less inclined to share, less inclined to render to either Caesar *or* God. Taxes and tithing seem no longer sufficient to serve man or praise God.

The result is bankrupt cities, bridges falling down, schools being closed, too much poverty, too few police. In Topeka, Kansas, there are not enough police and prosecutors to protect women from domestic battery. In my town – Vallejo – thieves are cannibalizing copper wire from city street lights. We are, it seems, no longer a civilized society.

As Judt warned:

> Something is profoundly wrong with the way we live today. For thirty years we have made a virtue out of the pursuit of material self-interest: indeed, this very pursuit now constitutes whatever remains of our sense of collective purpose. We know what things cost but have no idea what they are worth. We no longer ask of a judicial ruling or a legislative act: is it good? Is it fair? Is it just? Is it right? Will it help bring about a better society or a better world? Those used to be *the* political questions, even if they invited no easy answers. We must learn once again to pose them.[178]

But this fall, there is a fresh breeze in the air, wafting through the canyons of Wall Street and the intersection of Montgomery and Pine. A new generation is learning anew to pose those old questions.

And, in a church of empty pews and crumbling buildings, God's people – young and old – are asking new questions about old models that no longer seem to work. On the list-serve of the School for Deacons, for example, folks are asking questions like:

> How can the church preach - and act - prophetically, if it is beholden to the government, *any* government? Cowed into silence by fear of losing its tax deductible status?
>
> How can we do so, if our hearts are set not on souls in need, but on our rusting, crumbling, increasingly empty buildings?
>
> How can we succeed if we do not put our treasure where our heart is?

And, at the San Francisco Deanery meeting Saturday before last, there was lots of earnest talk about new models of doing church, of focusing on mission, rather than on buildings. Some of us have learned that you don't need buildings to do mission...that, if you build it - community - they will come...to worship Christ and support one another. I'm thinking, of course, of Open Cathedral in the Tenderloin, the Mission - and, hopefully soon, Lake Merritt - and of all the outdoor, outreach churches of Ecclessia Ministries...of Boston's Common Cathedral, of the Hip-Hop Mass in the South Bronx, and so many other examples of a church that lives and thrives because it does not conform to conventional wisdom or worldly expectations

I recall describing Open Cathedral at some church meeting on Nob Hill and being taken aback by a question: "How do you *monetize* that?" *Monetize* the Good News? Souls as commodities? People not as bodies and souls to be saved, but as "pledging units" to be hoarded? What kind of bottom line is that?

It is the bottom line not of a church of hopeful abundance, but one of fearful scarcity...of a church that promulgates, not a mission statement, but a business plan...of a church that, in this season of stewardship, seems to have forgotten the parable of the talents.

Fact is, we *are* monetizing Open Cathedral. Our expenses are minimal. Yes, we do have to pay our ministers, but there are no walls or ceilings to maintain, no utility bills. And our people are incredibly generous - the passing tourist from Florida who put a hundred dollar bill in my hand at MacAllister and Leavenworth, the homeless man who put seventeen cents into the offering cup on the corner of our altar, the kids who drove hundreds of miles from a walled church in Colorado to hand out the sandwiches they made, other youngsters from Tiburon willing to put their arms around those who would not be welcomed by their elders within their walls.

And we are not ashamed to beg. Didn't Francis? Didn't the Disciples? And people have responded - wealthy people who understand what a "fair share" is, some perhaps not so wealthy who are willing to make sandwiches for the hungry, the hundreds who write checks to the San Francisco Night Ministry...not because they need a tax deduction, but because they've heard and understood Matthew 25.

Actually, none of this is new. It is a very old model that pre-dates the regal basilicas of Constantine's official, privileged church...and of America's co-opted, tamed church. It is the church that meets in people's homes and coffee shops as covenant groups. It is the church that gathers in the open air in public places like Fernandez Park or a Home Depot parking lot. It is the church that dares to ask why the poor have no food, that seeks to emulate the first church of Acts - "the whole group of those who believed [who] were of one heart and soul" and who distributed what they had "to each as has any need."[179] It is the church that is not cowed by the IRS, by our coziness with power, or by our fear of getting our hands dirty in some distasteful way. It is the church that has not taken the talent it received and buried it in its undercroft, but put it to good use in our community.

It is way past time for that church - *our* church - to speak and act "unwisely," courageously, to seek a new model that is actually very old. I'm reminded, in this regard...in this season of stewardship, of Morris West's wonderful novel *The Shoes of the Fisherman*, of Anthony Quinn's Pope Kiril who was not afraid, as West put it, to "go out from Rome and travel like the first Apostles to confront the twentieth century," to sell the treasures of the Vatican to feed the starving millions of China, to "risk our worldly dignity to step down into the market place and proclaim the Unknown God."[180]

Won't you render unto that God, to such a church, some small portion of your treasure? It's the sort of church we're building together here in Pinole.

AMDG

WHAT THEN SHOULD WE DO?
A SERMON IN THE WAKE OF THE NEWTOWN MASSACRE
DECEMBER 20, 2012

And the crowds asked him 'What then should we do?'[181]

And, Friday morning, I asked myself "What then should *I* do?"

The night before, I had completed a fairly decent sermon. Before turning to the heavy stuff about good fruits worthy of repentance, our obligations to the poor, and our obligations to ourselves to experience what it means to be poor in spirit, I intended to have some fun talking about colors – the blue of hope, the rose candle of joy, the purple of repentance.

It was done. And I so looked forward to peace and quiet on Friday and Saturday – my first free Saturday in months – and a chance to catch-up… to write the cards and buy a tree and just dust and clear the clutter.

And, then, I turned on the TV and, sitting there numb, I asked myself "What, then, should I do…about Sunday morning…about this sermon?" I could ignore my pain and yours and deliver what I had written. I could pare it down, remove the lighter stuff, and offer the gist of what I had written… ignoring the nation's pain and all the flags at half-staff.

Then, I remembered another national tragedy – September 11. And I remembered the garden variety lectionary sermon the following Sunday, a sermon that didn't mention the tragedy or the grief we all felt. I remembered too how ill-served and angry I felt. For we had something we had to talk about and we didn't.

This sermon was published in the Vallejo Times-Herald, December 23, 2012.

We have something we have to talk about this morning and, with your permission, we will. I put away the sermon I had written and I will be brief in what I have to say in its stead. Then I'll do my best to listen, for I feel sure there are probably things you want to say. Where was God in all this? What do we tell our children? Remember Job? Why do bad things happen to good people? Why do the good die young? Why the little children, Lord, why the little children? Is there, indeed, evil in the world? I'll hang out in the sanctuary after coffee hour. We can continue the conversation here… or later. You know my phone number and e-mail address.

I'm talking, of course, about the killings in Newtown, in Portland, in Aurora, Milwaukee, Vallejo, and Richmond, Oakland and San Francisco; I'm talking about the 30 gun deaths every day, the 11,000 every year; about the 310 million guns on the loose in this country…one for every man, woman, and infant. I'm talking about our rampant incivility and our increasing proclivity to violence. And I'm talking about the absence of adequate treatment of mental illness.

Surveying such a scene, John the Baptist might well ask "Where are your good fruits worthy of repentance?" and, seeing far too few, declare us also a "brood of vipers."

What, then, should we do? Surveying the scene, our answer has, for too long, been "What *can* we do?" The guns are too many, the problem's too big, the forces arrayed against doing anything are too strong.

What kind of answer is that for a Christian, especially during this season of reflection, repentance, *metanoia*, turning around. Where is our resolve, our courage our hope.

What kind of answer is that for an American? Don't we still have a dream? Don't we always say "We can do it…*Si se puede!*"?

At long last, I think I heard the President say "Yes, we can!" and mean it. Wasn't there was a tear in his eye on Friday as he addressed the nation?

"As a country we have been through this too many times.
Whether it is an elementary school in Newtown, or a
shopping mall in Oregon, or a temple in Wisconsin, or a

movie theater in Aurora, or a street corner in Chicago -- these neighborhoods are our neighborhoods, and these children are our children. We're going to have to come together to meaningful action on this, regardless of the politics."[182]

Are we now ready to hold his feet to the fire and, regardless of the politics, take meaningful action about our culture of violence, about addressing mental illness, and, above, all about controlling the number and types of guns available and keeping them out of the hands of the hands of the violent and mentally ill.

We know well the politics of the issue and the specious nature of the arguments the NRA will again deploy. Isn't it time, however, for the church to find its voice and enter the fray to address the morality of the issue. Is this season of peace not an appropriate time for the church to speak out against this violence that breaks our peace and kills our children...against this national shame that is our out-of-control gun culture? Didn't we take the first tiny steps two years ago, approving a diocesan resolution banning guns in our churches and opposing California's open carry law?

And isn't it time for a sensible discussion about the Second Amendment. Hasn't America changed a bit in the 223 years since the Founding Fathers put pen to paper? Do we still need an armed citizen militia now that we have a National Guard? Do we still need guns to put food on the table or clear the land of Native Americans too stubborn to move?

John again confronts us from a distant wilderness with his shocking cry – "Wake up! Get on with it! Produce those good fruits worthy of repentance…fruits that will prepare the way of the Lord."

And how shall we answer? What then shall we do?

There are three things we should do. First, press the President and all politicians to do what they should do to end our national epidemic of gun violence. Second, pray for the victims, the survivors, and also for ourselves, for we too are victims. Take the hand of the person next to you and pray with me, as I share Friday's Shabat prayer by Rabbi Rachel Barenblat of Newtown:

God, let me cry on Your shoulder.
Rock me like a colicky baby.
Promise me You won't forget
each of Your perfect reflections
killed today. Promise me
You won't let me forget, either.

I'm hollow, stricken like a bell.
Make of my emptiness a channel
for Your boundless compassion.

Soothe the children who witnessed
things no child should see,
the teachers who tried to protect them
but couldn't, the parents
who are torn apart with grief,
who will never kiss their beloveds again.

Strengthen the hands and hearts
of Your servants tasked with caring
for those wounded in body and spirit.

Help us to find meaning
in the tiny lights we kindle tonight.
Help us to trust
that our reserves of hope
and healing are enough
to carry us through.

We are Your hands: put us to work.

Ignite in us the unquenchable yearning
to reshape our world

so that violence against children
never happens again, anywhere.
We are Your grieving heart.[183]
Amen
Now hug your children and tell them how much you love them.

AMDG

THE CITY THAT KILLS THE PROPHETS
A LECTIONARY SERMON FOR LENT TWO 2013

Jerusalem, Jerusalem, the city that kills
the prophets and stones those who are
sent to it![184]

It's good to be home. As most of you know, I've been on the road these past few weeks, visiting Ecuador…from the Amazon to the Andes…and, beyond, to the Galapagos. And, in Panama, I got to visit a century-old Canal and the isolated San Blas Islands. In both countries I got to know the indigenous people – the Hourani, Quiche, and Kuna – and the *meztisos* – black, and white and brown – who share in equal measure the blood and culture of Spain and Africa and those same indigenous people. And I got to experience – and celebrate – the wildest, widest diversity of flora, fauna, birds, and animals imaginable…thousands upon thousands, the good God made them all. They are experiences I long to share…stories I long to tell. Maybe after Lent.

Today, however, I want to talk about another part of the world. I want to talk about Israel and Palestine…and Jerusalem, the city that is the capital of both, the city that continues to kill the prophets and stone those who are sent to it seeking peace. It is another place I have visited recently and often. And I feel compelled to talk about it not just because Jesus does in Luke today, but because we at Christ the Lord have undertaken to share the love of Christ with the world…the *whole* world; because, in this, the holiest corner of the world, there is an acute shortage of love; and because, this month, we face another potential make-or-break point in the decades-long search for peace in the Holy Land.

For, in a few weeks, the President will arrive in Jerusalem. He does so, bearing an olive branch, talking reconciliation, and seeking the *Shalom* that is the peace that rests on justice. But he does so as injustice continues to be heaped upon injustice and as so many – Palestinians and Jews alike – have given up on the dream of two states living side by side in peace. We can only pray that he is not rebuffed by a stiff-necked and unwilling people and stoned like so many others sent to it preaching justice and seeking peace.

Such was the brutal fate endured by Jesus, scorned and killed by the Romans and Jews – occupiers and occupied - he sought to reconcile, the children he sought to gather together "as a hen gathers her brood under her wings." So it was in the time of Jeremiah, when Israel, threatened from the north, placed its faith, not in God and righteousness, but – foolishly, we know from history – in worldly military might. Such is the foolishness of hubris. It is the hubris that Jeremiah railed against, as Assyrians and Babylonians prepared their siege ramps against the walls of Jerusalem and that Jesus warned against as he wept over the city, saying, later in Luke, "If you…had only recognized on this day the things that make for peace."[185]

And this is not just an ancient story confined to Biblical times. For in our times – my lifetime – too many prophets, sent to Jerusalem seeking peace, have been killed within its walls or because they made the journey. In 1948 Count Bernadotte of Sweden was gunned down by Jewish terrorists as he sought to broker a cease-fire in Israel's war of independence. In 1951 Jordan's King Abdullah I was killed by Arab terrorists as he prayed at the Al Aqsa Mosque on Jerusalem's Temple Mount. In 1977 Egyptian President Anwar Sadat travelled to Jerusalem where he proposed peace to the Israeli Knesset. Two years later he signed the Camp David Agreement that cemented that peace…and, in 1981, paid the price Jerusalem always seems to demand of peacemakers… gunned down in Cairo by Egyptian extremists. In 1994 Itzhak Rabin and Yasser Arafat shared the Nobel Prize for signing the Oslo Agreement that set in motion what we know as the "peace process." The next year, Rabin was assassinated by a Jewish extremist as he spoke at an election rally in Jerusalem. And, a decade later,

Arafat was poisoned by God knows whom.

And, now, yet another decade later, the "peace process" they started lies dead in the water. The blood continues to flow. And the new young leaders in Jerusalem seem heedless to the lessons of history, numbed to injustice, and deaf to the voices of prophets both old and new. Puffed up again with their seeming military prowess, they find hidden to them those "things that make for peace." Heaping further injustice and indignity upon their Palestinian brothers and sisters whose land they've occupied for half a century, they wonder why peace eludes them and court the condemnation of present-day prophets who, like Jeremiah, warn that "This is the city that must be punished; there is nothing but oppression within her."[186]

But it is not pre-ordained that this must continue. Jesus today speaks not of punishment, but of his continued desire to gather together all the children of Jerusalem, indeed, all God's people, "as a hen gathers her brood under her wings." He speaks not in anger, but in sadness…and in hope… in the hope that those who rule in Jerusalem might turn from oppression and reliance on military might and seek, instead, justice and the ways of peace. And he speaks not just in a particular time and place, not just to Herod, but for all time and to all who have wandered from that path. And, as has become clear to the most casual observers, the current rulers in Jerusalem have strayed dangerously far from the path of justice and peace. There is an urgent need for them to hear the sadness and longing in Christ's voice and to heed the warning implicit in his message.

It is time for the church to speak in that voice and to deliver to the leaders of Israel the prophetic message they must hear. It is time for the friends of Israel to cease being enablers and to speak with love the truth that brings salvation.

Unfortunately, at this critical moment, the church – our church – has lost its voice and hunkered down in fearful, shameful silence. Last July, at General Convention, it was urged to condemn the illegal Israeli settlements on the West Bank and to boycott their products. It refused to do so. At the urging of the Presiding Bishop, it also refused to listen to the voice of

Palestinian Christians in their 2009 *Kairos Document* or even to undertake a study of their plight. And her signature was conspicuously absent from the October letter from the leaders of fifteen churches – Lutherans, Methodists, Presbyterians, UCC and others – urging Congress to hold Israel accountable for its actions.

Dismayed, a dozen leaders of the Episcopal Church – a pantheon of my spiritual heroes...bishops like Ed Browning, Steven Charleston, Leo Frade, and Gene Robinson; our National Cathedral Dean Gary Hall; and dear Bonnie Anderson, our most recent Past President of the House of Deputies – used Martin Luther King's Birthday to issue a "Prophetic Challenge to the Executive Council of the Episcopal Church." Supported by South Africa's Desmond Tutu and New Zealand's Jenny Te Paa, they urged our Executive Council to join the other fifteen churches in seeking accountability from Israel for the $3.1 billion it receives annually from the United States. That letter, now signed by over four hundred Episcopalians, myself included, was presented to the Executive Council on Thursday. I've posted the full letter on the bulletin board and will make it available electronically so that you might read it in its entirety. Let me now read the few paragraphs that are the powerful prophetic heart of its message:

> Just as this church stood with South Africa and Namibia during the dark days of Apartheid, so we recognize that we need to be standing with our sister and brother Palestinians who have endured an Apartheid that Archbishop Emeritus Desmond Tutu has described as worse than it was in South Africa. All peoples who have experienced oppression, including indigenous peoples who have known what it is to be dispossessed of their land, understand the Palestinian issue.

> Israel must be held accountable for allowing an occupation for 45 years that suffocates the dreams of freedom that Palestinians hold every bit as much as African Americans sought on that day when Dr. King told

the world that he had a dream. Occupation cannot be justified as a tool of security. Occupation is its own form of violence, a prescription for frustration and rage among those shackled under its harsh restraints…

As elected leaders of The Episcopal Church, we ask Executive Council to:

- Immediately send a message to Congress that the Episcopal Church supports our 15 ecumenical colleagues, who include the church leadership of the Lutheran, Presbyterian, Methodist, and United Church of Christ denominations, that wrote to Congress October 5, 2012, calling for accountability of Israel's use of foreign aid from our government. The voice of The Episcopal Church is woefully missing in the request our colleagues made to Congress.

- Immediately move forward with our Church's corporate engagement policy so that our financial resources are not being used to support the infrastructure of this suffocating occupation.

- We respectfully ask for a public accounting of the Executive Council's work on these matters no later than the meeting of Council June 8-10, 2013.[187]

The Executive Council, which will meet next week, has placed the letter on its agenda. I pray that it will heed its call.

That said, I recognize that not all of you may agree it or with me. Not all of you may be convinced that the Palestinians' dreams of freedom are being suffocated or that the church needs to be standing with them. Having stood in their midst and having experienced the conditions under which they live, however, *I* am convinced. But I cannot command *your* conviction or expect you to be persuaded by this or any sermon.

I can, however, expect you to look anew at the situation in Israel/Palestine with fresh eyes – with the "open hearts, open minds" we envision ourselves as having. I can ask you to read, not just this letter, but also the plea of Palestinian Christians in their *Kairos Document*. I can suggest that you check out the study guide – *Steadfast Hope* – prepared by the Episcopal Peace Fellowship…and perhaps consider forming a study group. Some of you might even be moved to consider a trip to the Holy Land – to Israel and Palestine. I would love to introduce you to some of my friends there – Christians, Jews, and Muslims – who are working for peace. I would love to walk the cobbled streets of Jerusalem with you and show you not just the holy sites, but also the settlements, the refugee camps, and the Wall that separates Jerusalem from Bethlehem…that separates the city where Jesus was born from the one where he was killed.

At that intersection of past and present, you too might cry out in despair "Jerusalem, Jerusalem, the city that kills the prophets and stones those who are sent to it!" You might despair of those who put their faith in "Iron Domes" and targeted assassinations and cannot see the humanity of the Other.

But, in that very humanity - of both peoples - and, indeed, in the city's very stones, I think you would find the stuff of hope…hope for a better future. Jerusalem, after all, was not just the city where Jesus was killed. It was the city where Christ was resurrected.

AMDG

THE POOR YOU ALWAYS HAVE WITH YOU
A LECTIONARY SERMON FOR LENT FIVE 2013

'*The poor you always have with you*'[188]

Most of us, I'm sure, are familiar with the term "proof-texting"… that dishonest art of plucking a word or phrase – out of context – from the Bible and using it to exclude some people, put down others, tout one's own righteousness, and, generally, use the word of God to justify one's own prejudices.

Sometimes some so-called Christians – the sort who give Christ a bad name – don't even need a **word** to justify their prejudices. There's no room in their churches for gays or lesbians…or me. Women? Obey your husbands and shut your mouth. And don't even think about the ministry. Preaching the Gospel? That's for men.

Trouble is, Jesus never uttered a single word about homosexuality and certainly said nothing that denigrated women or in any way excluded them from ministry.

So what did he talk about? Think about it. Were you to take a red letter Bible and do a 'wordle" of everything in red – you know, the words that Jesus actually spoke – you'd come up with something like this – money, rich, poor, wealth, poverty, charity, justice.

Jesus spent an awful lot of time talking about money…about how too much causes spiritual difficulties for the rich, about how too little causes physical problems for the poor, and about the good society in which there is an equitable distribution of the resources of the community.

And, make no mistake about it, Jesus was very clear about where he stood on all of this. His was not the Prosperity Gospel that comes out of

Tulsa and fills our TV screens – a Gospel in which wealth is an outward sign of righteousness and God's favor. No his was and is the Gospel in which the poor are blessed and the marginalized are welcomed.

And it is for reason that our reading this morning from John is so problematic. The church's well-filled and self-satisfied proof-texters latch onto that last sentence, pluck out that phrase "the poor you always have with you," and conclude that there's nothing we can do – nothing we need do – to alleviate poverty. And the rest of us are left to wrestle with a seeming contradiction to the overwhelming thrust of Jesus' teaching.

But, is it? A contradiction? Let's put these seven little words back into the story about the crowd at the house of Simon the leper and consider the events there in the context of the Passion of Christ that was about to play itself out over the next few days. Consider also how pivotal these events were in what was about to happen. Witness the fact that they are retold – nearly word for word - in three of the four synoptic Gospels.

Jesus, as we hear in John, had just raised Lazarus from the dead – his penultimate miracle, presaging his own Resurrection. This was no small stuff. This was no water into wine trick; no walking on water that some still try to attribute to hallucination; no healing the blind and lame, as other healers of the time had also reportedly done; not even curing the incurable, the lepers. No this was the raising of a dead human being. And it was not some feat of CPR or a near-death experience on some operating table. No, Lazarus had been dead for four days. As Mary, his sister, warned, he stank.

No wonder "many of the Jews...who had come with Mary and had seen what Jesus did, believed in him."[189] They believed, at last, that this was the Messiah. The crowds grew and they grew louder and the chief priests and Pharisees became alarmed. Mind you, Bethany is just a stone's throw east of Jerusalem and, I expect they could hear the noise echoing across the Kidron Valley. "If we let him go on like this, everyone will believe him and the Romans will come and destroy both our holy place and the nation"...to which Caiaphas replied "better...to have one man die for the people than to have the whole nation destroyed." "So," John tells us, "from that day on they planned to put him to death."[190] All they needed was someone to tell them where Jesus was, so they could arrest him. The die had been cast.

Enter Judas Iscariot, who, by John's telling, was already a conniving thief. In Mark's version, however, Judas was but one of several in the crowd who were scandalized by what they claimed was a wasting of the precious nard. Might he also have been alarmed like the Pharisees, personally weak, and fearful? "This is going too far! The Messiah! God! He's going to get us all killed!" For whatever his rationale, Judas high-tailed it to the Pharisees to volunteer his services in betraying Jesus. They had their man. The clock was ticking.

This, then, was the context of Mary's extravagance, Jesus' gratitude, and those words about the poor that have so often been twisted.

Consider Mary's actions. She was well-known to Jesus and, like Martha and their brother Lazarus, much loved by him. It was, after all, the tears of Mary that moved Jesus to perform this miracle that he must have known would be his death knell. And, close as she was to Jesus, Mary probably was, indeed, saving the expensive perfume for Jesus' burial. And, moved deeply by getting her brother back, why wouldn't she have thrown herself at Jesus' feet and poured the perfume on him in extravagant gratitude? Why is this not surprising? Would there be any limit to *your* gratitude, if, in response to a tearful prayer of yours, Jesus were to return a dead brother, mother, or child to you.

And would not Jesus – would not God – be moved to tears by love so reciprocated. Would not Jesus – our very human brother –chastise Mary's critics? "Leave her alone!" he says. And, in Mark, he adds "why do you bother her? She has done a good service for me."[191]

And the poor? Listen once again to Mark, to his more nuanced version of that much-misused passage – "Let her alone, Jesus says, "For you always have the poor with you, and you can show kindness to them whenever you wish."[192]

Far from telling us to ignore the poor, he was urging us once again to "show kindness" to the poor…to the poor who, in the phrasing of Deuteronomy, "would always be in the land"…and reminding us of the never-ending nature of the task. All he was asking for, in this instance, was for us to pause for a moment to honor the extravagant love of a grateful woman and, I would add, to imitate it by loving God with all your heart and mind and soul. And, in like fashion, whenever we wish – whenever we can – to show kindness to the poor.

Jesus was good Jew and he knew Scripture inside out. He was always quoting it, calling his fellow Jews not just to read the words, but to live their meaning. He knew well what he was doing here, invoking the words and meaning of Deuteronomy.

And the words and meaning of Deuteronomy are clear in this regard. The God of Deuteronomy did not beat around the bush. He issued commands. "There should be no poor among you.… If there is a poor man among your brothers in any of the towns of the land that the LORD your God is giving you, do not be hardhearted or tightfisted toward your poor brother. Rather be openhanded and freely lend him whatever he needs.… There will always be poor people in the land. Therefore I command you to be openhanded toward your brothers and toward the poor and needy in your land."[193] Yes, there will always be poor people - not always *them*, but sometimes *us* - and we must always share – and receive – openhandedly… not because those who have can look down on those who have not and offer a portion of their plenty, but because it is right and just to share. It is not a matter of *noblesse oblige* or feel good charity. It's a matter of justice. It's the way it's spozed to be. Haven't we been told "There should be no poor among you….?"

As Dom Helder Camara, that great Brazilian bishop and liberation theologian, once asked "When shall we have the courage to outgrow the charity mentality and see that at the bottom of all relations between rich and poor there is a problem of justice?"[194]

When indeed?! Looking around our own very rich country where "greed is good," where things are too often valued more than people, where so many are "hardhearted and tightfisted," one has to wonder, in sadness and outrage, "When indeed?!"

Every day the Dow Jones hits a new high…while 46 million of our brothers and sisters live in poverty. That's families of four scraping by on less than $23,000 a year, while Wall Street executives annually rake in individual salaries of more than $23 million. One percent of our people own 33 percent of our wealth, while 50 million of us go to bed hungry every night. And Congress seeks to reduce access to food stamps and WIC and Head Start to preserve the lowest tax rates ever for that one percent. Yes, we will always have the poor. They – perhaps *we* – are in every town of our land. And we're left to ask, in sadness and outrage, "What are we to do?"

Might we also ask that question we've been asking every Sunday this Lent and will again this morning: "What would Jesus do *now*?"

Might he, as Lutheran pastor Ken Wheeler has suggested, call "the collective Christian community to act with faith and boldness to turn the nightmare of poverty into a table where there is enough for everyone?"[195]

Might he, like Dr. Christopher Hughes of Doctors for America, have difficulty accepting the argument that "fighting poverty, including improving access to health care, better education and so on, must only be done on an individual, charitable basis?" Might he agree with Dr. Hughes that "that advocating for social justice and government intervention in particular, is appropriate?"[196]

What would Jesus do now? What will you?

Yes, we will always have the poor with us. But, God tell us, "There should be no poor among you"…and God commands us "do not be hardhearted or tightfisted," but be "openhanded"…until the poor are, at last, no more. *That* is the never-ending task of those would follow Jesus.

AMDG

A SHEPHERD SHOULD SMELL LIKE SHEEP
A LECTIONARY SERMON FOR EASTER 2013

One of the things I do in the diocese is to serve on our Commission on Ministry. Those who do so are assigned individual postulants to shepherd through what can be a daunting process. Appropriately enough, the postulants once called us shepherds. But what were the postulants called? Neither they nor we could bring ourselves to calling them sheep…as in, "Let me introduce you to Fred, my sheep." Awkward to say the least and, some would say, condescending. So, together, we became "companions." Get it? Commission on Ministry – COM – panions. Problem solved, we patted ourselves on the back for our sensitivity…and our questionable sense of humor.

So what is it about that term "sheep" that might be objectionable? To begin with, sheep have a reputation for being dumb…for often straying unwittingly into danger. That's why they need shepherds – to herd them in the right direction and keep them safe. Another way of looking at that is to say that they don't have minds of their own. They can easily be manipulated and led in wrong directions. Surely, you've heard how easy it is to lead a sheep to slaughter. That's why they need a *Good* Shepherd who will lead them instead to green pastures and still waters.

And let me remind you of one more thing about sheep – They smell. Ever been around a wet sheep? Ever put a pair of wet mittens on a radiator to dry? Ever put on a woolen sweater that hasn't been properly treated? I've got a lovely sweater from Scotland. But it smells like a barnyard and the lanolin still rubs off on me. Let's face it, sheep are smelly and greasy.

And those who hang around sheep also smell. That's a fact I was reminded of a few weeks ago, as I read Pope Francis' remarkable Chrism

Mass homily. Addressing his priests, but also all Christians, he spoke of the fragrant oil with which priests are ordained and with which we are all sealed in ministry at our Baptism. That oil, he said, "does more than simply lend fragrance to [the] person [anointed]; it overflows down to 'the edges.'"[197] "The Lord," Francis continued, "will say this clearly: his anointing is meant for the poor, the prisoners and the sick, for those who are sorrowing and alone."[198] These are words that reminded me of my own ordination vow "to serve all people, particularly the poor, the weak, the sick, and the lonely" and, I added under my breath, the marginalized, excluded, and oppressed. And they are words that should remind us all of our baptismal vows to "seek and serve Christ in all persons, loving your neighbor as yourself" and, seeking peace and justice, to "respect the dignity of every human being."

But they cannot remain just words. They are vows to act. They are vows to share the love of Christ with the world. As we heard last week, that requires us to show hospitality to those who walk through those doors and come to us. But it also requires us to go out those doors to those who are hurting, to go where they are and enjoy *their* hospitality. Sometimes it requires getting down into the trenches in some dark corners of the world and getting our hands dirty. As Francis said, "We need to 'go out,' then, in order to experience our own anointing, its power and its redemptive efficacy: [to go out] to the 'outskirts' where there is suffering, bloodshed, blindness that longs for sight, and prisoners in thrall to many evil masters." We need to "go out and give ourselves and the Gospel to others, giving what little ointment we have to those who have nothing, nothing at all."[199]

We need to "go out" and get up close and personal with those who are hurting…the way Francis washed the feet of a Muslim woman in an Italian prison Holy Thursday, the way others at ICE headquarters in San Francisco washed the feet of immigrants awaiting deportation, the way I've learned to hug my homeless brothers and sisters and pray with them for their survival on the street, the way I've learned to accept their prayers for me.

There is indeed a healing balm of Gilead, a balm we're called to share, but, in sharing it, we may come away reeking not of its pleasant fragrance, but rather of other more pungent odors. But, that's okay. It's the way it's spozed to be. As Francis reminded us in that Chrism homily, "A shepherd should smell like sheep."

But, sometimes that smell can offend the sensitive nostrils of those accustomed to the sweeter aromas of incense, those who would hide behind their walls and liturgies and hoard the precious oil for their own purposes. But, as Francis said, the beauty of liturgical things is "not so much about trappings and fine fabrics than about the glory of our God resplendent in his people" and the precious oil of anointing "is not intended just to make *us* fragrant, much less to be kept in a jar, for then it would become rancid … and the heart bitter."[200]

But, too many Christians have become just that – rancid and bitter – as they hoard their dwindling resources and watch their buildings empty. Capping their jar of healing oil and seeking to tame Jesus and squeeze him into a liturgical lockbox, they wonder where the newcomers are…and who will pay for the buildings. Frantic for newcomers – the sort that look like them and promise to behave like them and play by old unchanging rules, they turn to novelty, to tinkering around the fringes, to "emerging church" models that are too cute by half and still too focused on propping up an institution rather than serving a community. Too many such efforts are aimed at "growing the church" rather than helping those in need…at bringing people into our buildings rather than getting our people out of those buildings and into the streets where those in need are struggling. If we do the latter, the church will grow. If we don't, it doesn't deserve to grow.

To which Bishop George Packard, our former chief of chaplains, adds the following:

> There is no going back. You can't sit anymore in churches listening to stodgy liturgies. They put you to sleep. Most of these churches are museums with floorshows. They are a caricature of what Jesus intended. Jesus would be

turning over the money-changing tables in their vestibules. Those in the church may be good-hearted and even well-meaning, but they are ignoring the urgent, beckoning call to engage with the world.[201]

So, how do we do that? How do we engage with the world? Might we begin by listening? Listening for the cry of a hurting world? Listening for the voice of our Good Shepherd, who tells us again this morning: "My sheep hear my voice. I know them, and they follow me."[202]

Might we then follow that Good Shepherd – Jesus – as he walks - without pausing - to every corner of this hurting world? Might we emulate him and, like him, seek to comfort and heal the poor, the weak, the sick… the lonely, the marginalized, excluded, and oppressed…those possessed of the demons of addiction and mental illness, the runaway teens, the closeted sexual minorities, the migrants seeking honest labor, the refugees, the sex workers, those who go to bed hungry or anxious and those who have no bed…and, yes, the sin-sick tax collectors and wounded centurions of our day entrapped in a society they represent but no longer understand? Might we walk with Jesus and, like him, share the precious ointment of our love with "those who have nothing, nothing at all." Might we, like him, walk with courage through the porticos of our temples and the corridors of secular power and remind the powerful of their obligations to the least among us…obligations they've too long forgotten?

Might we live into the words of a song Peter[203] probably sang on the way to Santiago de Campostela and that we sing at the West County Detention Center with migrant families? It's called "Caminando con Jesus"…"Walking with Jesus." If I could play a guitar and sing like Mother Susan, Jeff, or my friend Francisco Herrera, we'd start singing right now and walk right out that door with Jesus to all God's lost sheep.

As Henri Nouwen tells us: "Our faithfulness will depend on our willingness to go where there is brokenness, loneliness, and human need. If the church has a future it is a future with the poor in whatever form."[204]

Returning here each Sunday to rest, to offer communal praise and thanksgiving, to seek strength and sustenance for the continued journey, will our works testify to us? Will we smell like sheep? I hope so, for I think, in the end, it will be by that smell – a good and fragrant smell to a Savior who awaits us as the Lamb of God – that Jesus our Good Shepherd will know us as his own and gather us to his side.

So, go out! Keep on walking!

AMDG

ENDNOTES

1 John le Carre, "Afterword," *Harper's Magazine*, April 2013, p. 63

2 Dr. Martin Luther King, Jr. (per Vincent Harding), "Beyond Vietnam" sermon, Riverside Church, April 4, 1967

3 Micah 6:8

4 Matthew 5:6

5 Walter Rauschenbusch, edited by Paul Rauschenbush, *Christianity and the Social Crisis in the 21st Century* (New York: Harper One, 2007, p.55)

6 King, "Letter from the Birmingham City Jail," April 16, 1963

7 Pope Francis, Chrism Mass Sermon, March 28, 2013

8 Albert Einstein, words engraved on the Einstein Memorial, National Academy of Science, Washington, D.C.

9 Bonnie Anderson, Past President, Episcopal House of Deputies, at a Grace Cathedral forum, San Francisco, October 19, 2008

10 Morris West, *A View from the Ridge: The Testimony of a Twentieth-Century Christian* (San Francisco: Harper San Francisco, 1996, p. 117). West, an Australian Roman Catholic and critic of his church, was the author of *The Shoes of the Fisherman*, the first in his Vatican trilogy, and several other novels.

11 Obery Hendricks, Jr., *The Politics of Jesus* (New York: Doubleday, 2006, p. 165)

12 Martin Niemoeller. *From U-Boat to Pulpit* (Chicago: Willett, Clark & Company, 1937)

13 Nikos Kazantzakis, *Report to Greco* (New York: Simon and Schuster, 1965, p. 512)

14 Jan Morris, *Conundrum* (New York: Harcourt Brace Jovanovich, Inc., 1974, p. 59). Morris, the accomplished Anglo-Welsh historian and travel writer, began life as James and has written more than thirty books under both names, the most prominent titles being *Pax Brittanica, The World of Venice, and The Matter of Wales*. She and her beloved Elizabeth remain married and I had the pleasure of visiting with them in their lovely home in Treffan, Wales in August 2001, the weekend of their son's wedding.

15 Kazantzakis, op. cit., p. 512

16 From the examination in the Ordination of a Deacon, *The Book of Common Prayer*, p. 543

17 Matthew 25:40

18 Isaiah 58:6

19 Don Stuart, *I'm Listening as Fast as I Can*

20 As cited in Zildo Rocha, Helder, *O Dom: uma vida que marcou os rumos da Igreja no Brasil* (Helder, the Gift: A Life that Marked the Course of the Church in Brazil), (Editora Vozes, 2000, Page 53)

21 William Sloane Coffin, *Credo* (Louisville, KY: Westminster John Knox Press, 2004, p. 66)

22 As quoted in *Sojourners* magazine. Houselander (1901-54), a Roman Catholic mystic, wrote several books, most notably *Reed of God* republished by Ave Maria Press in 2008

23 In my Jesuit high school – Fordham Prep – we included these letters at the end of every paper. They mean *Ad Majorem Dei Gloriam* or "For the Greater Glory of God" – words that strike me as an appropriate way to end a sermon.

24 Luke 9:57

25 Francis Thompson, *The Hound of Heaven* (Mount Vernon, NY: The Peter Pauper Press, nd)

26 Nikos Kazantzakis, *Report to Greco* (New York: Simon and Schuster, 1965, p. 186)

27 Ibid, p. 243

28 John Masefield, *The Collected Poems of John Masefield* (London: Heinemann, 1923)

29 Psalm 139

30 Isaiah 40

31 Henri Nouwen, "Waiting for God" in *Watch for the Light: Readings for Advent and Christmas* (Farmington, PA: Plough Publishing House, 2002, p. 31

32 Mark 1:41

33 Leviticus 13:45-46

34 Hendricks, op. cit., p. 159

35 Ibid, p. 160

36 Ibid, p. 165

37 As quoted in *Sojourners* magazine. Honan, a UCC minister, founded the Grace Street Ministry in Portland, Maine. He writes about his experience in (Kobo, 2012)

38 Isaiah 6:8

39 Abraham J. Heschel, *The Prophets: An Intoduction,* (New York: Harper Torchbooks, 1969, p. 12). This and the following citations of Heschel are from "What manner of man is the prophet," the introductory chapter of the book.

40a John 10·14

40b John 10:16

41 Martin Luther King, Jr. interview with Alex Haley, *Playboy*, January 1965

42 King, Q&A after speech at Western Michigan University, Kalamazoo, Michigan, December 18, 1963

43 Bishop Eugene Robinson, statement to the Episcopal Church House of Bishops, March 11, 2008

44 1 John 3:17

45 John 11:33

46 Mary Oliver, "What I Said at Her Service" in Mary Oliver, *Thirst* (Boston: Beacon Press, 2006, p.19)

47 John 11:33-35

48 John 11:47-53

49 John 11:44

50 Eugene O'Neill, *Lazarus Laughed* (New York: Boni & Liveright, 1927, p. 148)

51 Ibid, p. 22

52 Ibid, p. 23

53 Ibid, pp. 23-24

54 John 20:30-31

55 John 20:30

56 Mark Braverman, *Fatal Embrace: Christians, Jews, and the Search for Peace in the Holy Land* (Austin, TX: Synergy Books, 2010)

57 Acts 5:28

58 Braverman, remarks at Bay Area Sabeel Conference, "A Time for Truth, A Time for Action: Palestine/Israel & the U.S. at the Crossroads," First Presbyterian Church of San Anselmo, March 5-6, 2010

59 Ibid

60 Zygmunt Bauman, *Modernity and the Holocaust* (Ithaca, NY: Cornell University Press, 1993, p. xii)

61 Luke 12:49

62 Walter Wink, *The Powers That Be: Theology for a New Millennium* (New York: Galilee Doubleday, 1999, p. 90)

63 Edwin Markham, *The Man with the Hoe and Other Poems* (New York: Doubleday and McClure, 1899, pp. 15-18). Republished many times and readily available in paperback.

64 Rauschenbusch, op. cit., p. 68

65 Ibid, p. 55

66 Leonardo Boff, *Ecclesiogenesis: The Faith Communities Reinvent the Church* (Maryknoll, NY: Orbis Books, 1997, p. 43)

67 Walter Brueggerman, *Sojourners* blog (sojo.net), August 2010

68 Jeremiah 4:25-26

69 Bruce Springsteen, "My City of Ruins"

70 Ezekiel 37: 4-6 and 12-14

71 Jeremiah 4:22

72 George W. Bush, Remarks at the Islamic Center, Washington, D.C., September 17, 2001

73 John 18:38

74 Johnny Cash, "What Is Truth"

75 Albert Einstein, letter to Josh Winteler, 1901

76 Einstein, cf. footnote 8

77 Samuel Ruiz Garcia, "In This Hour of Grace," Pastoral Letter, August 6, 1993, in John Womack, Jr., *Rebellion in Chiapas: An Historical Reader* (New York: The New Press, 1999, p. 237. A copy was delivered to Pope John Paul II during his August 11-12 visit to Izamal, Yucatan. His response in an August 11 speech there was a warning to those (like Ruiz) ministering to the indigenous people that "interests that are foreign to the Gospel cannot be allowed to sully the purity of the mission that the Church has entrusted to them" (ibid, p. 236). A crackdown followed.

78 Acts 10:42

79 Ibid

80 The Baptismal Covenant, *The Book of Common Prayer*, p.304

81 Matthew 5:13

82 Kazantzakis, op. cit., p. 186

83 Bauman, op. cit., p. 206

84 Ibid, p. 207

85 Nick Kristoff, "Watching Thugs with Razors and Clubs in Tahrir Square," *New York Times*, February 2, 2011, p. A27

86 "Tis the Gift To Be Simple," The Hymnal, 554

87 Isaiah 58:6

88 Psalm 95:10

89 Psalm 95:8

90 Mahmoud Darwish, *Unfortunately It Was Paradise: Selected Poems* (Berkeley, CA: University of California Press, 2003, p. 7)

91 Kazantzakis, op. cit., p. 243

92 Braverman, op. cit., p. 114

93 Ibid, p. 115

94 Genesis 12:2

95 Leon R. Kass, *The Beginning of Wisdom: Reading Genesis* (New York: Free Press, 2003, p. 257)

96 Ibid, p. 258

97 John 4:22

98 Psalm 95:10-11

99 Deuteronomy 4:23-24

100 Ibid

101 Matthew 5: 9 and 11

102 Matthew 10:40

103 L. William Countryman and M.R. Ritley, *Gifted By Otherness: Gay and Lesbian Christians in the Church* (Harrisburg, PA: Morehouse Publishing, 2001)

104 Robin Hodson and Shireen Miles (eds.), *Telling Our Stories* (Sacramento, CA: Episcopal Diocese of Northern California, 2002, p. 11)

105 Galatians 3:28

106 William Shakespeare, *The Merchant of Venice*, Act III, Scene I, 60-68

107 Matthew 15: 25-26

108 Matthew 15:24

109 Matthew 15:12

110 The author's dog and the church mascot at Christ the Lord

111 Ecclesiasticus (Sirach) 44:1-10

112 The Lord's Prayer

113 Simon Wiesenthal, *The Murderers Among Us* (New York: McGraw-Hill, 1967)

114 Simon Wiesenthal, *The Sunflower: On the Possibilities and Limits of Forgiveness* (New York: Schocken, 1997)

115 Actually, the source for this is Sura 5:32 of the *Holy Qu'ran*

116 Eva Fleischner, commentary in *The Sunflower,* p. 140

117 Abraham Heschel, commentary in *The Sunflower*, pp. 165-166

118 Ibid, p. 166

119 Matthew Fox, commentary in *The Sunflower,* p. 146

120 Theodore Hesburgh, commentary in *The Sunflower*, pp. 163-164

121 Langston Hughes, "Harlem (2)" in Hughes, op. cit., p. 426

122 Romans 12:19

123 Katharine Jefferts Schori, sermon at St. Paul's Chapel, New York, September 11, 2011 (www.trinitywallstreet.org)

124 Rodney King, televised plea for peace during Los Angeles riots, May 1, 1992 (See: abcnews.go.com/US/video/rodney-king-16589937)

125 Psalm 100:3

126 Ezekiel 34:12-16

127 Ezekiel 34:18

128 Matthew 25:35-40

129 Obery Hendricks, op. cit., p. 9

130 Matthew 25:34

131 Peter J. Gomes, op. cit., p.165

132 Lynette Wilson, "Day of Action Marks 60 Days of Occupy Wall Street," Episcopal News Service, November 18, 2011 (See: http://archive.episcopalchurch.org/79425_130553_ENG_HTM.htm)

133 Ibid

134 Ibid

135 1 Samuel 3:8

136 Mark Sisk, statement on events at Duarte Square, December 16, 2011 (http://episcopaldigitalnetwork.com/ens/2011/12/16/new-york-bishop-presiding-bishop-issue-statements-on-ows/)

137 Katharine Jefferts Schori, statement on events at Duarte Square, December 16, 2011 (http://episcopaldigitalnetwork.com/ens/2011/12/16/new-york-bishop-presiding-bishop-issue-statements-on-ows/)

138 Marc Handley Andrus, "Occupy Dispatch #2", www.bishopmarc.com, December 20, 2011

139 Martin Luther King, Jr., "Letter from Birmingham City Jail," April 16, 1963

140 Ibid

141 2 Kings 2:13

142 Henry Smith Leiper, "From Pulpit to Prison," in Martin Niemoeller, *From U-Boat to Pulpit* (Chicago: Willet Clark & Company, 1937, p. 205

143 Ibid

144 John 12:23-26

145 Tim O'Brien, *The Things They Carried* (New York: Broadway Books, 1998)

146 Thomas a Kempis, *My Imitation of Christ* (Brooklyn, NY: Confraternity of the Precious Blood, 1954). This was the copy I carried in Vietnam.

147 Ibid, p. 361

148 Martin Luther King, Jr., "I've been to the mountaintop" speech in support of striking sanitation workers, Memphis, April 3, 1968

149 Oscar Romero, penultimate homily, March 23, 1980

150 Oscar Romero, interview with *Excelsior*, Mexico City, March 10, 1980

151 Oscar Romero, penultimate homily, March 23, 1980

152 Oscar Romero, final homily, March 24, 1980

153 Acts 4: 34-35

154 Acts 4:32 and 2:46

155 Acts 2:47

156 2 Samuel 7:6

157 Richard Helmer, "The Church as Institution: Life or Death." Episcopal Café, July 4, 2012 (http://www.episcopalcafe.com/daily/episcopal_church/the_church_as_institution_life.php)

158 Richard Helmer, "Structure and Budget: Gaining Perspective," Episcopal Café, July 7, 2012 (http://www.episcopalcafe.com/daily/general_convention/structure_and_budget_gaining_p.php)

159 2 Samuel 7:11-13

160 Ephesians 2:20-21

161 Ephesians 2:14

162 Bonnie Anderson, opening remarks at 77th General Convention, Indianapolis, July 4, 2012, Episcopal News Service (http://episcopaldigitalnetwork.com/ens/2012/07/04/general-convention-opening-remarks/)

163 John Lennon, "Imagine," The Beatles

164 Proverbs 1:20

165 Genesis 1:27

166 Proverbs 8:22-30

167 Andrew Seeley, "What Is Wisdom?" Thomas Aquinas College, 2000 (http://www.thomasaquinas.edu/news/dr-andrew-seeley-"what-wisdom")

168 Wisdom of Solomon 7:24

169 John 1:1-5

170 Wisdom of Solomon 8:1

171 Proverbs 1:20-22 and 32

172 Proverbs 30:8

173 Commonly attributed to Emerson, some claim it a misattribution. See: http://emerson.tamu.edu/Ephemera/Success.html

174 Mark 12:17

175 Josephus, *Antiquities of the Jews*, XX 8:8, 9:2

176 This quote from a 1904 speech by Holmes is engraved above the entrance to IRS headquarters in Washington, D.C.

177 A British-born writer and professor of European history, Judt authored or edited fourteen books and was a frequent contributor to the *New York Review of Books*. He moved to New York where he served as director of NYU's Erich Maria Remarque Institute. A secular Jew, raised as a Zionist, he became an out-spoken critic of Israeli policies vis-à-vis the Palestinians. He died in 2010 of ALS. *Ill Fares the Land*, one of his last books, published that year, was an impassioned defense of social democracy and attack on the return of unbridled capitalism.

178 Tony Judt, *Ill Fares the Land* (New York: Penguin, 2010, p.2)

179 Acts 4:32 and 35

180 Morris L. West, *The Shoes of the Fisherman* (New York: William Morrow and Company, 1963, p. 370)

181 Luke 3:10

182 Barack Obama, remarks at White House press conference, Washington, D.C., December 14, 2012

183 Rabbi Rachel Barenblatt, Love InshAllah blogspot, December 14, 2012 (http://loveinshallah.com/2012/12/14/god-let-me-cry-on-your-shoulder/)

184 Luke 13:34

185 Luke 19:42

186 Jeremiah 6:6

187 "A Prophetic Challenge to the Executive Council," as posted on the Episcopal Peace Fellowship blogspot, January 18, 2013 (http://epfnational.org/PIN/a-prophetic-challenge-to-the-executive-council/)

188 Mark 14:7

189 John 11:45

190 John 11:48-53

191 Mark 14:6

192 Ibid

193 Deuteronomy 15:4ff

194 Dom Helder Camara as quoted in Ken Wheeler, "The Poor You Will Always Have With You," January 10, 2012, Living Lutheran blogspot {http://www.livinglutheran.com/blog/2012/01/you-will-always-have-them-with-you.html#.UdtbXDbn-Uk)

195 Wheeler, Ibid

196 Dr. Christopher Hughes, "The Poor You Will Always have With You," Doctors for America blogspot, May 11, 2011 (http://www.drsforamerica.org/blog/the-poor-you-will-always-have-with-you)

197 Pope Francis, Chrism Mass homily, Rome, Italy, April 5, 2012

198 Ibid

199 Ibid

200 Ibid

201 George Packard as quoted in Chris Hedges, "The People's Bishop," TruthDig bolgspot, May 7, 2012 (http://www.truthdig.com/report/item/the_peoples_bishop_20120507/)

202 John 10:27

203 Peter Champion is the husband of the author's vicar at Christ the Lord, Susan Champion. He is also a priest.

204 Henri Nouwen, Verse of the Day. Verse and Voice, Sojourners blogspot, April 9, 2013 (http://sojo.net/blogs/2013/04/09/voice-of-the-day)